S0-AEU-277

PRAISE FOR
FEARLESS

"Charlene Ligon inspires the reader to look for "Evelyn T. Butts" in the dictionary under *FEARLESS*. Too often the story of women especially black women is untold or under reported in the civil and human rights success movement. *FEARLESS* captures the essence of brilliance and sacrifice of Mrs. Butts and her drive to make the world better for her family, her community, her nation. I appreciate how Ligon does not shy away from recognizing men like Jordan, Dawley, and Holt who valued Mrs. Butts as a peer and a leader while refusing to hide the chauvinism and sexism that too often hindered progress. Another volume on Evelyn Butts & The Women of Virginia's 3rd Force is in order. Read *FEARLESS* and have your faith restored in the power of one to make a positive difference for millions. No Evelyn Butts; no Governor Doug Wilder; no President Barack Obama!"

—RODNEY A. JORDAN, Chair, Norfolk School Board

Rodney is a nephew of Butts' Attorney and friend Joe Jordan and is the first elected Norfolk School Board member to serve as chair.

"*FEARLESS* ought to be required reading for every high school student in Virginia. It is the inside story of the struggle for basic American rights, told from the perspective of those who lived through the oppression and fought for change. Any discussion of the impact of the poll tax or civil rights in Virginia, would be incomplete without an understanding of the life and accomplishments of Evelyn Butts."

—CHUCK ROBB, former Virginia governor
and former US senator

Norfolk Mayor Kenneth Cooper Alexander, in his foreword for the book, said of Evelyn Butts, "What she accomplished as a voting rights champion truly spans the generations and deserves our continued recognition."

—KENNETH COOPER ALEXANDER,
Mayor, Norfolk, Virginia

FEARLESS

How a poor Virginia seamstress took on Jim Crow, beat the
poll tax and changed her city forever

Charlene Butts Ligon

Smallwood Charlotte Press
Bellevue, Nebraska

Copyright © 2018 by Charlene Ligon

All rights reserved. No part of this publication may be reproduced, distributed or transmitted in any form or by any means, including photocopying, recording, or other electronic or mechanical methods, without the prior written permission of the publisher, except in the case of brief quotations embodied in critical reviews and certain other noncommercial uses permitted by copyright law.

HARDCOVER: 978-0-9993836-0-5
PAPERBACK: 978-0-9993836-2-9

Charlene Butts Ligon/Smallwood Charlotte Press

www.evelyntbutts.com

Charlene Butts Ligon. -- 1st ed.

Library of Congress Cataloging in Publication Data is available.

For my sisters

Lillie Jeanette Brinkley and Patricia Ann Stevenson

For the grandchildren

Cheryl Brinkley-Smith, Augusta Carballo, Tonya Hill

Jimmie Ligon, Evelyn Ligon-Moton and Robin Ligon

Struggle is a never ending process. Freedom is never really won,

you earn it in every generation.

--Coretta Scott King

CONTENTS

FOREWORD

If there were a Virginia Civics Hall of Fame, the late Evelyn Thomas Butts, a native of Norfolk, Virginia, would be one of its most esteemed inductees. She was best-known for her 1960s federal lawsuit that abolished the poll tax for state and local elections, an onerous device that had suppressed the voting power of poor blacks and whites throughout the South for several decades. Relentless in her work to strengthen our democracy, Mrs. Butts also helped register new voters by the thousands, and she stood steadfast in drawn-out fights for improving low-income neighborhoods and integrating Norfolk's public schools.

Mrs. Butts achieved her landmark victory at the U.S. Supreme Court on March 24, 1966, and she died in 1993, but it is vital that we continue to learn about her life, contributions and legacy. For those lessons, we can now turn to the first book-length biography of Mrs. Butts, *FEARLESS:* How a poor Virginia seamstress took on Jim Crow, beat the poll tax and changed her city forever, written by her youngest daughter, Charlene Butts Ligon.

In *FEARLESS,* we see Mrs. Butts as a mother and active citizen who works tirelessly to improve the lives of family members and neighbors, while also joining or leading battles against discrimination in employment, public schools, neighborhood services and voter access. She is a poor seamstress who makes most of the clothing worn by her three daughters, and she is the primary caregiver for her husband, Charlie Herbert Butts, a disabled Army veteran of World War II.

FEARLESS is not only a loving remembrance of Mrs. Butts but a testimony to the essential roles that civic activism, grassroots leadership and persistent community organizing play in keeping our democracy vibrant and healthy. Indeed, Charlene Ligon notes that she hopes that her book serves as "a blueprint for today's activists so they may follow in (her mother's) footsteps to become influential figures in local politics, and not be deterred by poverty or social status or competition." While much of *FEARLESS* involves activities in Norfolk, Virginia, a careful reading of the book should prompt ideas on how the experiences and lessons from the life of Evelyn Butts could apply to struggles in many communities across our nation.

For example, when the Supreme Court struck down the onerous poll tax, Mrs. Butts and her supporters did not stop there. They stepped up their energies to register and educate voters. That, in turn, helped lead to the election of civil rights attorney Joseph A. Jordan Jr. to the Norfolk City Council in 1968, the first African American council member since the Reconstruction era of the late 1800s. Other personal and community milestones followed, including Mrs. Butts being appointed to the powerful board of commissioners of the Norfolk Redevelopment and Housing Authority. There also were setbacks, and Mrs. Butts was often cantankerous. But Mrs. Butts persisted, and her great works continue to bear fruit – and I am proud to be part of her legacy.

Think about it. Knocking down the poll tax and registering thousands of new voters over the years were key steps toward Norfolk finally electing an African American as mayor – my election in May 2016, which was 50 years after Mrs. Butts' landmark victory at the Supreme Court. *FEARLESS* deepened my appreciation for the profound impact Mrs. Butts had on our community and nation. What she accomplished as a voting rights champion truly spans the generations and deserves our continued recognition.

Charlene Butts Ligon provides historical context throughout *FEARLESS*. As she observes, black men gained voting rights after the Civil War (women, back then, did not have voting rights), and voters elected dozens of black citizens to a wide range of local and state offices. But political advancement dissolved with the end of Reconstruction and, as Mrs. Ligon writes, "The erasure of black electoral participation in Virginia was not an accident." Virginia even reshaped its state constitution in 1901-02, adding the poll tax among other discriminatory measures. Leading politicians did not hide their intent. As noted in Encyclopedia Virginia, state Sen. Carter Glass, a leading force in the 1901-02 convention, declared that the purpose was "to eliminate every Negro voter who can be gotten rid of, legally, without materially impairing the numerical strength of the white electorate."

Other Southern states also imposed poll taxes as part of a package of repressive laws, "a general scheme of disenfranchisement," historian Frederic D. Ogden writes in his classic study, The Poll Tax in the South. "Additional restrictive provisions were lengthy residence, registration, and literacy." Virginia's poll tax was $1.50 a year, pocket change in 21st century America but a hurdle for the poor decades ago, especially when the law stipulated that it had to be paid for three consecutive years before an election. Thus Ogden characterizes Virginia's poll tax as the most "burdensome" because of its combination of "poll tax rates, coverage, time of payment, and proof of payment."

In Virginia, there were other attempts to end the poll tax before Mrs. Butts raised her challenge; however, they had failed. On the national level, the 24th Amendment to the U.S. Constitution, ratified in 1964, banned poll taxes for federal elections but did not include any wording about state and local offices. The lawsuit filed by Mrs. Butts in 1963 was combined with one from several residents of northern Virginia and went to the Supreme Court as *Harper v. Virginia State Board of Elections.* The 6-3 decision struck down poll taxes as the high court proclaimed that "a state violates the Equal Protection Clause of the Fourteenth Amendment to the U.S. Constitution whenever it makes the affluence of the voter or payment of any fee an electoral standard. Voter qualifications have no relation to wealth."

While the 1966 victory lifted the burden of poll taxes from millions of low-income citizens, the decision continues to reverberate. Political historian Alexander Keyssar, in his comprehensive The Right to Vote: The Contested History of Democracy in the United States, writes that "From a broader, more historical standpoint, the case's significance was far greater and less technical: almost two centuries after that nation's founding, economic restrictions on voting had been abolished in all general elections."

Progressive lawyers are building upon the work of Mrs. Butts and the 1966 poll tax victory by suggesting that affluence also should be removed as a barrier when running for office. "We face a new wealth barrier in our elections: the exclusionary campaign finance system which allows big money interests to dominate our politics and drown out the voices of ordinary citizens. ... The poll tax story reminds us that a sustained people's movement combined with continued pressure in the courts can eradicate an entrenched and anti-democratic system. The wealth primary barrier may stand today. But, it will not stand forever," voting rights attorney John Bonifaz wrote in Abolishing the Wealth Primary: The New Poll Tax in American Politics, an article published on March 24, 2016, to celebrate the 50th anniversary of the Supreme Court decision.

On that day, Norfolk also commemorated the victory and the courage of Mrs. Butts. Now, thanks to Charlene Butts Ligon's book, *FEARLESS*, we are reminded why it is important to keep celebrating the life of Evelyn Thomas Butts. Our lives and communities are so much better because of her.

Kenneth Cooper Alexander
Mayor, Norfolk, Virginia
October 27, 2017

CHAPTER ONE

INTRODUCING EVELYN

Evelyn Thomas Butts stood in the plaza outside the United States Supreme Court in Washington, D.C., on a cold and windy day in January 1966, waiting for an Associated Press photographer to take her picture. With the wind chill, the temperature felt like fifteen degrees. She was wearing a black coat she had made herself. Every garment she wore that day was put together on the sewing machine she kept on the enclosed front porch of her two-bedroom house in Norfolk, Virginia.

She had one black dress for formal occasions. She wore a hat given to her by her sister Estelle, whom her family called Bunky—a soft faille hat with a band around it, both stylish and effective against the cold. Every woman in her family had borrowed the hat at one time or another, and she wore it in Washington as a good luck charm.

Most days, Mrs. Butts could be described as a seamstress, an African-American woman approaching middle age, a mother of three daughters, and the wife of a 100-percent disabled World

War II veteran. But on this day, she was the plaintiff in a lawsuit against the Commonwealth of Virginia, arguing that its poll tax discriminated against poor persons like herself. That's why the Associated Press wanted her picture.

The photographer positioned her off the building's right-front corner, and crouched low as he tripped the shutter. In the resulting photo, the Court's columns loom high behind her. Mrs. Butts is not looking into the camera, but gazing off into the distance, as though she had somewhere to go. She is not smiling. It's a pose one might expect of a corporate CEO. She looks powerful.

And she was. I know this because Evelyn T. Butts was my mother. My two older sisters and I had front-row seats to many of the moments that led up to this photo. At the time it was shot in 1966, we were all grown and ready to start our own lives. In a sense, this photo, and her victory in the high court case that had brought her to Washington, amounted to something like her society debut. From that point on, my mother was an important political figure in Norfolk, and remained so until the last years of her life.

She never graduated from high school. She never held elected office, though she ran three times for a City Council seat. She earned no salary from her political activism, which she undertook for decades. All was volunteer work. Still, she had clout. In her late sixties, just months before she died, a white Republican running for office came to her hospital room to ask for her endorsement. That moment says much about her place in Norfolk. Once, when asked how she'd become so prominent a public figure, she said, "I just have feelings for other people. I feel for others, and their circumstances, and always try to help them when they are having problems."

When she died in 1993, the Virginia Senate adopted a resolution calling her "one of the most influential political leaders of the last three decades." She was honored for eliminating the poll tax, registering nearly 3,000 voters in one six-month period, and leading a political organization that shaped Norfolk politics and helped elect both white and black candidates for a generation. The senators also lauded her twelve-year service as an unpaid city housing commissioner, as the Democratic Party's Second Congressional District chair, and as a member of various city commissions and boards.

"Her outstanding accomplishments notwithstanding," the resolution read, "Evelyn Butts' most lasting legacy lives on in the entire generation of political leaders, both black and white, who owe their success to the tireless and inspired efforts of a Norfolk seamstress who overcame great odds to become an influential and successful community leader."

In 1995, one of the main thoroughfares in our Norfolk neighborhood, Elm Avenue, was renamed Evelyn T. Butts Avenue. I spoke at the dedication ceremony. It was held outdoors in front of the Oakwood Chapel Church of Christ, on a cold day. My mother had been a force in the neighborhood for more than forty-five years, since a time when political activism was not safe for a black person in a Southern city. During the summer of 1954, two months after the school desegregation case *Brown v. Board of Education* was handed down, bombings had shaken a neighborhood called Coronado, about a half-mile from our house. The bombings were intended to spur black families who had recently purchased homes in Coronado to leave. I live in a mostly white neighborhood south of Omaha, Nebraska, and cannot imagine having moved there while bombs were going off. Yet my mother and her contemporaries found the courage to ignore violent opposition to their quest for economic equality and civil rights.

Many people in attendance that day in 1995 were senior citizens, friends of my mother. They withstood the cold for an hour, listening to speeches, to pay their respects to her. Inside the church there is a tribute wall with newspaper articles and photos of my mother. Many bus lines terminated at Elm Avenue, so when I visit Norfolk today, I am always reminded of my mother because so many city buses have placards reading "Evelyn Butts" in the destination slots over their windshields.

These honors do not, however, tell the entire story of my mother's complicated relationship with Norfolk. She also knew failure and great disappointment. In the 1980s, a new generation of activists, captivated by Jesse Jackson's Rainbow Coalition, turned away from the political organizations my mother founded. It caused a rift in the black community and the city's Democratic Party. When my mother was voted out of Concerned Citizens by its remaining four members, she retired from politics. Journalist Earl Swift of the *The Virginian-Pilot* wrote in a piece commemorating her life, "Evelyn Butts' career had become a Shakespearean tragedy: She'd dived from the heights of power to something very close to irrelevance.

"This was someone who should have finished life celebrated, rather than forgotten," he wrote, ending the article: "History better be kind to this woman. Evelyn Butts was important."

Our family agrees. In 2007, my sister Jeanette Brinkley and I began compiling material for a book about our mother. Our oldest sister Patricia Stevenson had died four years before. In 2017, during the writing of this manuscript, Jeanette died from complications of diabetes and heart disease, leaving me, the youngest, to complete the task for all of us. In some ways, researching my mother's life has made me think about her in ways I had not while I was growing up under the same roof. Who was Evelyn Thomas Butts? What gave her such confidence? How could she be so determined when she was beset with never-ending problems, both personal and in her community? Where did her incredible strength come from? It is my hope that a new generation of Democratic activists will study her life and search for their own answers to that question. I want others, similarly challenged, to find inspiration in my mother's story so that they, too, will take on political challenges great and small and be motivated, like she was, by compassion and a desire to help others.

***

My mother began her life on May 22, 1924, in Norfolk, a port city dominated by a mammoth military complex, and located at the mouth of the Chesapeake Bay in southeastern Virginia. She was the third child born to Lottie Cornick and George Washington Thomas, who had met in Norfolk and married there in 1918. Beginning the following year, they had six children, one boy and five girls: Julia, Walter, Evelyn, Rosanna, Mary Frances, and Estelle.

Granddaddy was from a small North Carolina town called Edenton, and moved fifty miles north to Norfolk to find work during World War I. A metropolitan area with military installations promised Granddaddy work as a laborer, and later in construction. Early in their marriage they lived on Union Street, near the downtown Elizabeth River waterfront. In Norfolk's colonial days, Union Street had been a place where slaves were sold and jailed. It's likely that their apartment could be described as a tenement. The young couple had five of their children while living there.

As was typical of Southern cities, Norfolk was segregated, with black neighborhoods scattered in pockets. The greatest concentration of African Americans was along a major north-south thoroughfare, Church Street, which was lined by black-owned movie theaters, clothing stores, restaurants and bars. Union Street met Church near its south end, putting the Thomases near the black community's cultural and mercantile heart.

In 1929, Granddaddy moved the family to New York City in search of better-paying work. He found it, too: During construction of the Empire State Building, there was a high demand for laborers, and Granddaddy worked on the landmark until it was completed in April 1931 then moved on to other building projects. Grandmother had her hands full with the children, the first five of whom had been born two years apart. When they arrived in New York, Julia was nine, and Walter, or "Tippy," seven. Mama was five, Rosanna was three, and Mary Frances, or "Pudney," wasn't even walking.

My grandmother had relatives in the city who put up the entire family until they got on their feet and moved into their own Manhattan apartment. It was there that my mother started school. Most of the other students were white, and she was liked and accepted by them. That experience formed her consciousness about the possibility of harmony and equality between the races.

Tuberculosis was endemic in New York, and in 1933, a year after my grandparents had their sixth child—Estelle, or "Bunky"—my mother's oldest sister, Julia, contracted the disease. She was confined to a sanatorium, and died later that year, at fourteen. My grandmother visited Julia in the sanatorium, putting herself at risk of infection. Perhaps as a precaution, she sent the older children to live in a home while she and my grandfather took care of the baby Estelle in the apartment. My mother did not remember much about the place where she and her siblings were sent. She said they had to take a ferry and she got seasick on the crossing, so it may have been located on Staten Island. The other memory she had was eating oatmeal every morning. She hated the oatmeal because it was slimy. After Julia's death, my mother and her siblings returned to live with their parents.

As it happened, my grandmother's devotion to Julia had, indeed, stricken her with TB, so George moved the family back to Norfolk in 1934. My grandmother's sister, Rosa Lee, and Rosa Lee's husband, Lucius White, owned two houses next door to each other on Sixth Street in Oakwood, an unincorporated community in semi-rural Norfolk County, north of the city. As in New York, my mother and her siblings were segregated to prevent them from exposure to the bacteria that causes TB. They lived with "Aunt Roz" while Granddaddy stayed with Grandmother in the house next door. Aunt Roz's daughter Lizzie and her husband also lived with her, in an addition that the family had built for them. Aunt Roz helped Granddaddy take care of her sister, washing all dishes and laundry she touched with boiled water, to sterilize them.

Aunt Roz was very religious and attended the First Church of Christ Holiness. She didn't wear lipstick and dressed modestly. Every night she listened to the evening news on the radio, and allowed the children to listen only to religious music. But when she was away, the girls would turn the dial to stations that played Billie Holliday, Louis Armstrong, and Duke Ellington. As soon as they heard the streetcar, they turned the radio off before Aunt Roz could catch them—heaven forbid—dancing.

Rosa Lee White was also quite the entrepreneur. She was a realtor and owned a corner store. While no political activist, she understood the issues, voted in every election, and encouraged her friends and neighbors to do likewise. In those days only white people ran for office, and it was essential to elect those with a kinder disposition toward the black community. Over the years, my mother absorbed Aunt Roz's values about the importance of politics, though she never acquired her passion for religion.

The Thomas children lost their mother on the last day of November in 1934. She is buried in the Calvary Cemetery on the Lafayette River, a cemetery for blacks. The siblings had endured much hardship in those early years of the Depression. They'd moved to a huge new city, stayed in a cramped apartment, were separated from their sister who died in their absence, and watched their mother become ill. They'd left New York City schools, where they experienced some measure of integration and friendship with white people, and returned to Norfolk—only to be separated from their mother again as her health collapsed.

My mother never spoke about my grandmother's funeral. She and her siblings moved out of Aunt Roz's house and in with their father next door. Though Granddaddy labored to take care of his family, my mother always thought of herself as an orphan after her mother's death, perhaps because she became the female head of the family. Because she was the oldest girl— though only a fifth-grader—it became her job to look after her three sisters, the youngest of whom was just two, and to cook for the whole family. Fortunately, my mother found herself surrounded by Oakwood women who kept large vegetable gardens and were wonderful cooks. They would teach her how to work magic in a kitchen.

The houses on Sixth Street were walking distance to the old Oakwood School, which served only black children in first to eleventh grades, there was no twelfth grade in most of the county schools. Tippy, Mama's older brother, did not stay in school long enough to graduate. Though he was extremely close to my mother, he felt compelled to return to New York City to find work. Perhaps he wanted to help provide for his siblings, as my mother was doing. Tippy lived with relatives in New York and sent money home to the family until he signed up to fight in World War II. I'm sure he sent money home while he was in the service.

In tenth grade, my mother met a boy named Kenny. Romance between them bloomed. She became pregnant, and Kenny's grandmother sent him away to North Carolina. My mother delivered their baby at Aunt Roz's house in July 1939, attended by a midwife. She named their baby girl Patricia Ann, and— feeling deep shame about getting pregnant before she was married—did not return to high school that autumn to complete her education. Kenny wrote love letters from North Carolina, promising to come back and make everything all right. He did visit after the baby was born, but stayed in North Carolina for two years while my mother suffered the embarrassment of raising their daughter as a single teenager. By the time Kenny came back, she'd decided that she did not want to marry him, after all.

Patricia Ann became everybody's baby. After she was born, all four Thomas sisters moved in with Aunt Roz. My mother was always a bossy older sister, but Rosanna, Pudney and Bunky loved her. She made sure her sisters graduated from the Oakwood School. No sibling was going to drop out on her watch. Aunt Roz's son and his wife needed a place to stay, so they moved into the house next door. My grandfather moved into a nearby rooming house nicknamed the Big House. It had probably been a plantation house at one time, and had a two-story, wraparound porch. Some of the small houses in the neighborhood were probably servants' quarters built during the days of slavery.

When Patricia was about two years old, my mother met Charlie Butts, a Virginia-born steelworker who was seventeen years her senior. He was one of eight children born to John Butts, and Lillie Britt, a farming couple in rural Sussex County, about one hundred miles west of Norfolk. At eighteen he'd moved with the family to upstate New York, near Buffalo, where he and his father found work in the steel industry. Now he was returning to Virginia after nine years' work in a steel mill in Lackawanna, and moved in with his cousin Howard and Howard's wife, Helen, one block from Aunt Roz's house. Howard and Helen introduced my mother to their dashing cousin. And that, as they say, was that.

Daddy was a good-looking man, with straight black hair and a well-trimmed mustache. He and Mama were the same height— five-foot-seven—though Daddy was slim, and Mama voluptuous. He was a jack-of-all trades, talented with his hands. They married in 1941, and rented a house four blocks north of Aunt Roz's place. The house had a shotgun layout, with a living room up front that opened onto a hallway. A bedroom branched off the corridor, which ended in a rear kitchen. An outhouse stood in the back yard. A hand pump inside the house drew water from a well down below. Their first daughter, my sister Lillie Jeanette, was born in the house in 1942.

The following year, when my father went to fight in World War II, my mother rode the streetcar downtown to work in the kitchen at Ames and Brownley, an upscale department store with a tea room. It was the only commercial cooking job she'd ever have. In those days black people worked out of sight as cooks and dishwashers, while white waitresses served the white customers. Aunt Roz watched the girls on the six days per week my mother worked at the department store and cleaned houses. My grandfather gave up on the Big House, which was dilapidated and scary, and moved in—giving my mother one more mouth to feed.

Somehow, she found time to join the Oakwood Civic League, an organization that gave the neighborhood's residents a forum for discussing life there, and ways they might see it improved. Oakwood was rustic. Its houses relied on well water, which was thick with minerals and often left rust stains in sinks and baths. All had septic tanks, which required periodic and expensive emptying. The streets were surfaced in dirt or gravel, and lacked curbs, gutters and sidewalks. The civic league pushed for piped water, connection to sewer lines, paved roads. Its meetings brought Mama out of the house and into the world of public debate for the first time. She found it suited her. She found she was good at it—incisive, well-organized, and unafraid of speaking in front of others. She found her voice. And before long, thanks to her humble start in that civic league, she found herself occupying a much larger role in public affairs than she'd ever imagined.

Meanwhile, my father was serving in the Army, and stationed in New Guinea. He wrote home often, and my mother saved all of his letters. He was in the 839th Engineer Battalion, operating and maintaining diesel and gasoline-powered shovels and running a bridge crane. In 1945 he returned to the States with a Purple Heart, having sustained shrapnel wounds in his back as the result of a blast. He convalesced in a hospital in Louisville, Kentucky, for seven months before making his way home. My mother was now the mother of two small children, the de facto mother to her three younger siblings, and the wife of a disabled veteran. She was twenty-one.

When he returned to Norfolk, my father walked with a distinctive limp. He and Mama bought the little shotgun house they'd been renting, and for a while Daddy was able to work at the Norfolk Naval Air Station despite his injuries. But eventually his disability intensified, and he could no longer work full-time. He supplemented his small pension by doing odd jobs around the neighborhood.

I was born in November 1948 in Norfolk Community Hospital, a facility that catered to the city's black population. I have to wonder how my parents got to the hospital, as we didn't have a car. They certainly didn't take the bus, so I assume my father's cousin Howard drove them. Both of my sisters had been born at home, delivered by midwives. Perhaps because Daddy had been in the military and was still working on the base, he could now afford the hospital. In any event, I was supposed to be a boy named Charlie. Mama liked to tell me that Prince Charles was born in England on the very same day. "If we were in England, the Queen would have given us one British pound because every baby born on that day got money from the Queen," she told me.

I slept in a crib in my parents' room. Patricia and Jeanette slept on a pull-out sofa in the living room. And my father and his cousin Howard built Granddaddy a little one-room house in the back yard, like Henry David Thoreau's at Walden Pond. It had a wood stove, so he could stay there even in the wintertime, which was fine by him—he preferred his privacy, even cooking some of his meals on that stove. We relied on pioneer technology in our own kitchen. To boil water, my mother had to build a fire in the kitchen stove, and we had an ice box that she cooled with blocks of ice. She was determined, once I was born, to buy a gas stove and a refrigerator. There were no gas lines in the street, so she had the stove hooked to a propane tank. I'm quite sure they went into debt to buy those appliances.

My mother returned to work at Ames and Brownley a few months after I was born. Every morning, she walked my sisters and me four blocks to Aunt Roz's house to drop us off for the day. At some point, she left the department store to work for two sisters, the Lamberts, as a domestic. They paid her four dollars a day. Eventually, she asked for a raise to five dollars. The sisters gave her the raise, but had her work four days a week instead of five, to keep her weekly pay the same. Mama eventually quit that job, but she continued to iron on Saturdays for a woman named Mrs. Brown. Then, rather than continue to ride the bus to the homes where she worked as a domestic, my mother decided to work at home as a seamstress. She already made all the clothes we wore, so she began to sew for others as well.

When I picture my mother, even in my earliest memories, I see a big woman. After giving birth to three children she grew stout and pillowy, and her size was part of her personality. She had a big voice and a big laugh to go along with her girth, and under the right circumstances she could come across as intimidating. She knew it, too. She did not mind that people in and outside the family called her bossy. But Evelyn Butts was also, and perhaps more memorably, caring and nurturing. She knew when to be bold and when to be soft. It was a rare gift.

Annie Nickens, the president of the civic league, asked Mama to attend a NAACP meeting at the Hunton YMCA, the branch for blacks in downtown Norfolk. Joining the NAACP would change her life in ways she could not have dreamed at that first meeting. Five days before Mama turned thirty, on May 17, 1954, *Brown v. Board of Education* was decided, establishing segregation in public schools as inherently unfair and unlawful. The NAACP legal team, under the direction of Thurgood Marshall, had argued the case before the U.S. Supreme Court. The nine justices were unanimous in finding the "separate but equal" approach to educating the races to be a violation of the Fourteenth Amendment to the Constitution, which guarantees "equal protection of the laws" to all Americans.

Norfolk's black newspaper, the *Journal and Guide*, published a syndicated article explaining the Supreme Court decision and hinting at the future. "Segregation of whites and colored children in public schools has a detrimental effect upon the colored children," the story quoted Chief Justice Earl Warren as saying. "The policy of separating the races is usually interpreted as denoting the inferiority of the Negro group, and a sense of inferiority affects the motivation of a child to learn."

"To separate (black children) from others of similar age and qualification solely because of their race generates a feeling of inferiority as to their status in the community that may affect their hearts and minds in a way unlikely ever to be undone."

The Court put off until its subsequent term taking any action on the order to desegregate. The first case, which would come to be known as *Brown I*, was a monumental cultural shift, overturning the 1896 precedent that had established "separate but equal" as a fulcrum of Southern society in the prewar twentieth century. The second case, *Brown II*, would leave it up to the states to determine how to put the law into effect, but famously encouraged them to tackle desegregation "with all deliberate speed."

When Brown was handed down, my oldest sister, Patricia, fifteen years old, was attending an all-black Catholic high school. She had previously been bused fifteen miles away to a public black high school in Chesapeake; my parents had scraped together money for tuition at St. Joseph's so she could attend school closer to home. My twelve-year-old sister, Jeanette, was attending Oakwood Elementary. I was six years old. Thanks to the Brown decision, I might have the opportunity to attend an integrated public school with children of various races, as my mother had experienced in New York City in the 1930s.

FEARLESS

At the age of sixty-five, Mama described her New York schooling to historian Tommy Bogger. "On the East Side school, they
treated me like I was a piece of chocolate. Everybody wanted to
play with me, you know, so I never feared that white folks would
want to hurt me, because where I attended school they loved
me. So when I came back here and got grown, I had no fear of
white people, because I thought that they all loved me like they
did when I was going to school up there."

Nothing in Virginia's history could justify my mother's opti-
mism. But without it, she might never have left the house.

CHAPTER TWO

THE CITY THAT CREATED HER

"All politics is local," as the late Democratic Speaker of the House, Tip O'Neill, once said. My mother's political career bears out that nugget of wisdom. She rose to prominence by working with her neighbors, tackling big issues on an intimate scale. And her story can be understood only through the lens of the locality where it occurred.

When I was in school, we studied the history of Virginia beginning in first grade. Because I went to all-black schools with black teachers, we also studied black history long before it became part of the curriculum in white schools. The history of my home state perfectly illustrates that you cannot write or speak of America divorced from the issue of race, and I cannot write about my mother without explaining the place she called home.

"Virginia" once encompassed what's now the entire eastern United States north of Spain's Florida. It had its start with three small ships from Britain's Virginia Company leaving London five days before Christmas in 1606. The roughly one hundred Englishmen in the expedition were out to make their fortunes with a settlement near "the bay of the Chesapians." They were not the first Europeans in the region—the Spanish had explored the Chesapeake Bay nearly forty years before—but earlier visitors had not fared well. Most had vanished without a trace, and the Spanish had given up any ambition to establish a colony in the bay they called "Bahia de Madre de Dios," or Mother of God.

The English were nonetheless wary of Spanish intentions, and when their ships sailed into the mouth of the Chesapeake Bay in April 1607, they passed through one of the world's greatest natural harbors in search of a protected site for settlement. As they maneuvered up a waterway they would name the James River, they rounded a promontory and sighted just such a place: an island hugging the north bank, bordered by deep water. They called it Jamestown.

The Virginia Company traded and fought with their neighbors, the Algonquin Indians, almost from the start, and at several junctures the outpost seemed sure to fail. But a decade on, Jamestown was beginning to thrive as a tobacco-based economy, with a population numbering around one thousand people. In 1619, the Virginia Company voted to establish a legislative assembly called the House of Burgesses. That same year, a ship carrying "twenty and odd" Africans, apparently captured from a Portuguese ship on the high seas, arrived in Jamestown. Records indicate the passengers were from an urban area in Angola. Educated and baptized, the Angolans were not enslaved at Jamestown, but treated as indentured servants.

This liberal arrangement did not hold. Twenty years later, lifetime servitude would be imposed on Africans in Virginia, and in 1661, it became the first British colony to formally enact slavery for blacks. Virginia was ground zero for the rise of slavery in North America.

Our family does not know exactly when our ancestors arrived in Virginia to be sold into slavery. We do know that my mother's great-grandfather Smallwood, born in 1830, was owned by a white man named John Ackiss II. His ancestor, also named John Ackiss, was a colleague of George Washington, Thomas Jefferson and Patrick Henry, and served in Virginia's House of Burgesses from 1762 to 1792.

We know, too, that Smallwood married a fellow slave named Charlotte Cornick. They had eight children, four boys and four girls, among them mama's grandmother, Lydia, born in 1862. John Ackiss emancipated Smallwood and gave him thirty acres of land, which he passed on to his eight children. Our family has long speculated about why Ackiss bequeathed property to Smallwood. Perhaps they were father and son. We don't know. We do know that Smallwood's descendants eventually lost the thirty acres. Today, it is part of an exclusive residential neighborhood called Birdneck Point in Virginia Beach. Our family cemetery is located on Bobolink Drive, in a small grove of trees between a tee box and a fairway near the 15th hole at the Cavalier Golf and Yacht Club.

I have visited this small, simple graveyard. Smallwood and Charlotte Ackiss rest side-by-side. Smallwood's headstone reads: "A soldier in Company E 23rd Division of the United States Colored Troops of the Union Army." His former owner, John Ackiss II, fought for the Confederacy.

In 1882 my mother's grandmother, Lydia, married a man named George Cornick, who'd been born free to parents who had been enslaved. We believe he did some kind of work around Princess Anne County Courthouse and taught himself to read and write. He worked for a wealthy family, the Kellums, and would accompany a member of that family from the courthouse when he transported tax revenue for deposit in the bank. George was a skilled fisherman and operated his own fishing business at Lynnhaven Inlet, a break in the bay shore of what's now Virginia Beach. George and Lydia had nine children, including my mother's mother, Lottie, who was born in 1899. Many of their descendants still live in what's now Virginia Beach and Norfolk.

Present-day Norfolk was the site of an Indian town called Skicoak. By the 1640s, the Indians had been driven from the area, and vast English plantations produced cattle, sheep and hogs, in addition to a lucrative tobacco crop—all goods that were easily traded with ships bound for the West Indies.

In 1655, a proposal from London for "Regulating Trade and Establishing Places for Ports and Markets" was met with disdain by the plantation elite, who believed that building towns in Virginia would destroy their way of life. But soon enough, both England and the colony experienced heartache and upheaval. Bubonic plague struck London, stranding Virginia's tobacco in warehouses, awaiting shipment; the tobacco finally arrived in London in time for the Great Fire of 1666. A war with the Dutch brought warships to Chesapeake Bay to confiscate tobacco and burn ships. A succession of hurricanes damaged and destroyed buildings in Virginia and North Carolina. The fast-growing population was creating poverty: Indentured servants would work off their debt, then have to scrounge for survival. England dumped its criminals in the colonies. Armed protests by the disaffected would occasionally occur, and in 1676 a full-scale rebellion erupted. In England, James II was removed from the throne in 1689.

The upshot of this discord was that the colony began to rethink its rejection of towns and to consider the benefits of a more diverse economy. In 1691, Norfolk and Princess Anne counties were established, and construction of a courthouse began near the Elizabeth River, not far from the site of the sacked Indian town Skicoak. A town was platted, and all of its lots were sold and occupied by 1696.

Meanwhile, the number of blacks in Virginia gradually increased, from twenty-three in 1625 to three hundred in 1650. By the time Norfolk's first streets were laid out, the colony's black population numbered over 16,000, and it leapt from there—to 60,000 in 1740, and 210,000 at the start of the American Revolution. Blacks fought on both sides of the conflict. Some earned freedom through their service.

For a Southern town, Norfolk was unusual in that there were free blacks living among the enslaved. The quality of life in town was considerably higher than on a plantation. Occupations open to blacks included hauling, ferry operation, barbering, carpentry, barrel making, stonecutting, plastering, painting, and blacksmithing. Men could also be employed as sailors, pilots, sailmakers, oystermen and fishermen. Some worked in the nearby Dismal Swamp in the lumber industry. Women worked traditional jobs as cooks, seamstresses, laundresses, housekeepers, innkeepers, servers, nurses and midwives.

A 1793 slave rebellion on the Caribbean island of Santo Domingo washed up on Norfolk's shores. Hundreds of boats carrying 10,000 French-speaking refugees fleeing the violence needed to be accommodated in a town that had not yet recovered from a disastrous fire during the Revolutionary War. Norfolk was an ugly place, with foul air and mosquitoes rising from its ubiquitous swamps. It also had a reputation for bad drinking water. But, to their credit, Norfolk's residents opened their arms to the refugees. Some returned to France, while others made a new home in Virginia.

Blacks comprised 40 percent of Norfolk's population in 1800. A jittery white ruling class was terrified of a rebellion like that in the islands. As a result, a tsunami of new laws were passed, affecting both freedmen and slaves. Blacks could not testify against whites in court. Curfews were imposed, and slaves needed passes to leave their owners' property. Teaching blacks to read and write was discouraged, and eventually outlawed altogether. Slaves could not work in medicine, teaching, or engage in a trade, and were forbidden to get licenses as pilots or captains. No freed blacks could move to Virginia. Existing black residents had to register with the town clerk. And finally, in 1806, all freed blacks were expelled from the state, a law that was sporadically enforced, leaving those remaining in a state of constant anxiety. The Constitution and congressional legislation outlawed the importation of new slaves into the United States after 1808.

According to the research of Tommy Bogger, an archivist at Norfolk State University, slave auctions occurred in at least two places in Norfolk—on Union Street and in Market Square. The auctions had onsite jails to ensure enslaved persons could not escape. Because there was a surplus of slaves in the upper South and a shortage in the deep South, Norfolk became a major port for shipping human cargo southward. After stops in Baltimore, Washington, D.C., Alexandria and Richmond, slave ships would depart Norfolk for New Orleans. Ten ships left the city in 1828, carrying a total of 1,634 slaves.

On August 24, 1831, news of Nat Turner's slave revolt in Southampton County, just fifty miles to the southwest, sent Norfolk into paroxysms of fear. A group of seventy-five blacks killed fifty-one whites. Before the rampage was put down, Norfolk's town council appealed for help from navy warships and the army's Fort Monroe, across the harbor in present-day Hampton, and militia patrolled the streets. The state executed fifty-six slaves, including Turner; dozens of others were killed by vigilantes until the state interceded to protect them as private property.

The massacre ushered in a spike in the persecution of slaves and abolitionists, and as an excuse to violently intimidate freed blacks, many of whom abandoned their property and fled the state. New laws were passed forbidding ministers from preaching on the virtues of abolition, and outlawing blacks from meeting at night.

Nevertheless, many runaway slaves made their way to Norfolk's harbor, where they could try to secrete themselves on ships headed north. The Fugitive Slave Act of 1850, which compelled the return of runaways even in free states, made it imperative that escaping slaves reach Canada.

After South Carolina seceded from the Union, Virginia called a constitutional convention in February of 1861, voting not to leave. The siege of Fort Sumter by Confederates brought Virginia into the Civil War. Fort Monroe remained in Union hands throughout the fighting, and once the federals declared slaves to be contraband, sheltered thousands of fugitives.

President Lincoln was personally on hand two months later for the advance that put Norfolk in Union hands on May 9, 1862, and it remained under federal control for the rest of the war. Many whites left, many black refugees arrived, and in time Norfolk became a city of paupers. People died of starvation every day.

The Emancipation Proclamation of January 1863 opened the door for freed blacks to fight for their rights. Five months later, the War Department created the United States Colored Troops. My great-great grandfather Smallwood Ackiss, eighteen years old in 1863, left the plantation and headed to Norfolk to join the Army. By 1864, Fort Monroe had organized two black cavalry regiments, three infantry units and one light artillery unit. These soldiers fought major battles in Virginia, including the capture of the Confederate capital at Richmond and the skirmishes that ushered Robert E. Lee's surrender at Appomattox.

After surrender, the South transitioned from a state of war to a state of uncertainty. Norfolk's blacks organized and demanded the right to vote in city elections, but their votes were not counted and a government of former slaveholders was elected. Black leaders began a campaign for equal suffrage in advance of the constitutional convention. Several leading black residents collaborated on a tract—"The Equal Suffrage Address. Also an Account of the Agitation Among the Colored People of Virginia for Equal Rights"—that encouraged blacks to organize for the right to vote. Norfolk's black citizens were ready to assume the responsibilities and rewards of full citizenship.

Yet, two months after Appomattox, Union soldiers raided the city's black districts and attacked their residents with bricks, rocks and pistols. Blacks retaliated by attacking a soldier later that night and they, in turn, were attacked by troops. Soldiers who had been their liberators were now their oppressors. The teeming port city seemed destined for unrest.

Virginia's first black newspaper, *The True Southerner*, moved from Hampton to Norfolk, determined to be a force for uplifting the community. It proved an elusive goal. In April 1866, some three hundred black men and women marched in drizzle to peacefully celebrate a new Civil Rights Act promising equality under the law. Armed black war veterans were on hand to guarantee the parade's safety, but when an off-duty policeman tried to prevent the marchers from reading the act, then encountered two revelers holding fake pistols, then was startled by someone firing a blank, bloodshed ensued. The policeman cut a marcher with a sword, and the officer's neighbor opened fire—killing his own stepmother—before he was himself fatally wounded.

Two whites were dead, and a crowd of blacks was blamed. Seeking vengeance, armed whites, some wearing Confederate gray, killed two, prompting the local army commander to request Richmond to declare martial law. After three days of rioting, seven blacks were arraigned for the death of the policeman's neighbor. Six were later released and one was sentenced to eighteen years in prison. No arrests were made for the attacks on black citizens. A local newspaper, *The Day Book*, editorialized that the riots offered proof that blacks were unfit to govern the city or state. An article called blacks "semi-barbarous." *The True Southerner* saw its offices ransacked by a white mob later that year. Its publisher left town.

In 1867, Congress adopted a Reconstruction Act establishing five military districts in the South, and requiring Southern states to adopt new constitutions that allowed blacks to participate in civic affairs and to vote. In Virginia, whites who held federal office but aided in secession were disfranchised, giving blacks a slight majority of the vote. Norfolk's blacks made up almost 50 percent of the city's population of 19,000. Consequently, the city sent a white man and a black man to the constitutional convention of 1868; Norfolk County, too, sent a black delegate. All three men were Republicans.

Of 105 convention delegates, twenty-five were black. In the first election for Virginia Assembly, twenty-one blacks won seats, though the white Conservative Party held a majority, along with the governor's mansion and the state's congressional seats. Norfolk city government fell to the conservatives, as well, though some blacks and white radicals were elected. Gerrymandering consolidated most blacks into one ward and reduced the number of representatives from eleven to five.

The Fifteenth Amendment, adopted in 1870, mandated that black men had the right to vote. However, ex-Confederates regained their voting rights, and the black majority in Virginia dissolved. Federal troops left Virginia that same year. More importantly, for our story, a poll tax enacted in 1876 prevented many blacks from voting, and a second law to disfranchise those convicted of petty crimes further eroded the black vote. Norfolk nevertheless continued to elect black representatives to the state's House of Delegates into the 1880s. Virginia even elected a black Congressman in 1890.

Reconstruction was followed by a period Mark Twain dubbed "The Gilded Age"—years in which it seemed that serious social problems were gilded over with a thin layer of gold. Manufacturing and industry grew exponentially, creating great wealth for a few. This was the era dominated by men like John D. Rockefeller of Standard Oil, Andrew Carnegie of Carnegie Steel and the Wall Street Financier J. Pierpont Morgan. Norfolk prospered. Oyster shucking employed thousands of black laborers, and a fleet of small boats operated by black men fished the region's abundant waters. Black women and children picked millions of quarts of strawberries grown in the countryside just beyond the city limits. Norfolk elected a reformist Mayor from a new political party called the Readjusters, who crusaded for black political equality, better funding for public schools, ending police corruption, providing aid for farmers and small businessmen, and other concerns of the poor and working classes. The party succeeded in abolishing the poll tax, but didn't hold onto power for long. Conservatives, calling themselves Democrats again, worked toward creating a one-party state.

It was also an era for organizing. Leading black organizations included the Grand United Order of Tents, which grew out of the underground railroad. Women in the Tents provided burial and accident insurance and housing for the poor. A long, quiet campaign for a black cemetery succeeded, providing an alternative to the potter's field outside of town. The nation's first black YMCA opened in Norfolk. A high school with an integrated faculty called Norfolk Mission College opened in 1886, providing daytime and evening classes. Black and white women each formed chapters of the Women's Christian Temperance Union.

The Gilded Age gave way to Jim Crow. In 1896, the Supreme Court decided in *Plessy v. Ferguson* that "separate but equal" accommodations for blacks and whites were constitutional. Meanwhile, Norfolk's population grew more diverse, as immigration brought Italians, Greeks, Russian Jews, Austrians, Chinese and other newcomers to settle there.

My grandmother Lottie was born in 1899, the fourth child of George Cornick and Lydia Ackiss. She and her eight siblings were somewhat insulated from Jim Crow on the thirty rural acres that Smallwood Ackiss had received from his former owner. Several generations lived together on the property, farming and fishing on the waterfront. They had no idea that soon their idyllic life would crumble under the pressure of development.

Two wars in the quarter-century between my grandmother's birth and my mother's birth in 1924 transformed Norfolk into the naval powerhouse it remains to this day. The Spanish-American War in 1898, though only a few months long, would establish the United States' role in the world in the coming century. It ended Spain's colonial rule of Cuba, and ended with American territories in Guam, Puerto Rico and the Philippines.

Jim Crow laws codified separate neighborhoods for blacks and segregated seating on streetcars. Norfolk's black residents reacted with a boycott and an attempt to establish their own transportation company, both of which failed. A young man came to Norfolk in 1907 to work as the plant manager for a paper called the *Lodge Journal and Guide*, distributed in the black community by the Knights of Gideon. P.B. Young was an acolyte of Booker T. Washington, and believed in his theories of economic nationalism and self-sufficiency. Within three years, Young bought the paper and renamed it the *Norfolk Journal and Guide*. Over the next four decades, it would become the most influential black newspaper in the South, with subscribers all over the country.

Another race riot occurred in Norfolk on July 4, 1910, when heavyweight boxing champion Jack Johnson beat the "Great White Hope," Jim Jeffries. Enraged whites pulled blacks off streetcars and beat them; the city's leading white newspaper wrote that the riot arose out of "the insolence of jubilant negroes." Without aid from the authorities, blacks retreated to their segregated neighborhood and stopped the riot by forming a "human wall of defense." The experience drove home the notion that black survival depended on concerted action.

In 1914, the state directed its municipalities to emulate Baltimore by writing ordinances to ensure residential segregation. Norfolk's ordinance required white people to vacate "colored blocks," and vice versa. The new laws did not restrict whites from conducting business in the black districts, a situation which fueled resentment in the black community.

Meanwhile, the Great Migration was on. Between 1900 and 1920, an estimated 1.5 million blacks left the rural South for urban areas in search of employment. Norfolk's black population jumped from 25,039 to 43,943 in the ten years beginning in 1910, so that it comprised 37 percent of the city's total. Working class whites feared the spread of black neighborhoods, prompting officials to designate Corprew Avenue as a boundary between the two. Locals called it the dead line. In 1916, the new Booker T. Washington High School, exclusively for black children, was built near the line.

While the war spurred the economy, blacks were rarely hired for skilled positions in the shipyards or elsewhere, and several black unions formed. One was the Transportation Workers Association, which tried to organize black women working as domestics to strike for better pay. One white employer reported his cook to federal authorities, and the police chief threatened to arrest any "loafers" in the black community, including domestics, who went on strike. The National Association for the

Advancement of Colored People (NAACP) formed a chapter in Norfolk in 1917, and the *Journal and Guide* promoted it, encouraging its readers to join this organization dedicated to the proposition that American democracy could be redeemed for blacks. Marcus Garvey's United Negro Improvement Association (UNIA), which attracted the laboring class, also established a presence in Norfolk, advocating Garvey's belief that America would never change and that blacks were better off moving to Africa.

Their rise in influence coincided with a resurgence of the Ku Klux Klan throughout the United States. The Klan did not have a presence in Virginia during Reconstruction, but gradually emerged in Norfolk after 1921. A Klan rally at Fairmount Park in 1924 drew 35,000 people for fireworks, concerts and athletic contests. Fairmount Park was near our neighborhood, right on the streetcar line that linked Oakwood and the business district. Two years later, a musical based on "The Birth of a Nation" was staged at a big theater downtown.

The Klan was denounced by Norfolk's newspapers, but only grew bolder. In September, a caravan of seven vehicles carrying twenty-eight Klansmen traveled to a farm in rural Princess Anne County, where the black Catholic high school, St. Joseph's, was hosting a concert by the Negro Boys Band. They snatched away a priest and interrogated him about whether the school was integrated. He was released, but the county sheriff and commonwealth's attorney refused to investigate his kidnapping. The incident so outraged the Norfolk City Council that it adopted an ordinance making it unlawful to wear a mask.

This is a small, grainy snapshot of the world into which my mother was born in May 1924. Norfolk was, and is, a bustling city on a breathtaking bay that teems with wildlife, and with a great harbor and proud naval tradition. It was, and is, a city both international and provincial, urban and rural, vice-ridden and churchgoing, cruelly segregated and politely Southern. Hers was a community of hard-working black families who still believed in the promise of democracy, though they were crowded into rundown neighborhoods where most did not own their homes, and many would never find adequate work. It was a community that had organized for its own improvement since just after the Civil War, and continued to organize no matter the obstacles Southern society placed before it.

My mother was born around the time our family lost our ancestral land to developers in Virginia Beach. I often wonder why she did not leave. Why would she stay in the South, with all of its historical, cultural, legal, and murderous baggage? Why stay in a place where white people obviously did not want black people to succeed—or to succeed only so much?

And yet, I cannot imagine my mother living anywhere but Norfolk, Virginia. She was as much a part of that place as the dust beneath the street in front of our house. I suspect that two kinds of people bring about change: those who emigrate to make themselves a better life; and those who stay put, to improve the places where their families have roots. My mother was a member of the latter group. She lived and died in the place of her birth, despite its flaws—bending it to her will, to redeem it for the future of all Virginians.

CHAPTER THREE

WINDS OF CHANGE

In the summer of 1954, when my mother told me I was going to kindergarten at Miss Alberta's house, I told her I needed a book bag.

"You don't need a book bag in kindergarten," she said, trying to reason with me.

"Yes, I do!" I insisted. Maxine, my next-door neighbor, was two years older than me, a second-grader. She had a book bag and I wanted one, too. As the youngest child in my family I was a little spoiled, and did not give much thought to how my parents might pay for the things I wanted. Our father received a disability pension from his military service, which kept a roof over our heads, but did little beyond that. Mama supplemented his income by sewing and working as a domestic. Though she was not a regular churchgoer, she often sewed for people who attended the neighborhood's churches, especially around Easter. She found other customers through a dry cleaner and laundry within walking distance of our house. Cavalier Cleaners, which was owned by a white man named Harvey, had many customers at the Norfolk Naval Base. Between church clothes and uniforms, my mother had plenty of sewing to do, but her income never amounted to much. If people couldn't meet her asking fee, she accepted whatever they could afford.

We didn't have a car and our neighborhood, Oakwood, was in Norfolk County. It was, in those days, still very much "country." When I told my mother I needed a book bag, she walked to a bus stop about a block from our house and rode downtown, along the way crossing a wide slash of mud where the streetcar tracks had been pulled up. There was no shelter at the bus stop, only a sign atop a metal pole. The ride downtown was about thirty minutes. She must have spent hours on that errand for me, probably making her purchase at W.T. Grant's on downtown Granby Street. I remember seeing her when she got off the bus and I running down the street to greet her. "What's in the bag?" I asked. She smiled and showed me the red plaid book bag and a tablet with big lines so I could practice writing. The paper was ivory colored and thin, almost like recycled paper. She also bought me one fat pencil with an eraser. I hugged her so hard.

The public school did not include kindergarten, so my parents paid a few dollars a week to send me to Miss Alberta's. Miss Alberta lived on Johnston Road, a couple of streets away from our house. We walked there before nine o'clock every morning. On the first day, I carried my book bag and wore a new plaid dress my mother sewed for me. Five or six children from the neighborhood attended the makeshift school in her dining room. We stayed until noon most days, though sometimes Miss Alberta would babysit me in the afternoon if my mother was doing day work as a maid.

I started kindergarten a few months after the Supreme Court's decision in Brown. The case consolidated five lawsuits from Kansas, South Carolina, Delaware, Virginia and Washington, D.C. My mother was well-aware of the upcoming decision through her membership in the NAACP, whose legal department was representing the plaintiffs. She had joined the Norfolk chapter around the time she learned our neighborhood and all of the surrounding Tanner's Creek area was going to be annexed by the City of Norfolk in 1955. Everyone knew that annexation could bring better services—roads, city water, sewers and the like—but it could also mean that entire neighborhoods would be seized by eminent domain, torn down, and replaced with housing projects or unaffordable houses. The Norfolk Redevelopment and Housing Authority had initiated the first urban renewal program in the country, called Project One, which had already cleared hundreds of acres of squalid housing and relocated thousands of residents. My mother intended to have a say in the future of our neighborhood.

These two issues—desegregation of the schools and redevelopment of our neighborhood—permeate my memories of childhood. I watched my mother evolve from "Mama" into a political activist that other people looked up to. The NAACP served as a crucible for her innate talents as an organizer. It was also a great social outlet. Many of her closest friends volunteered with the organization.

One of the most significant relationships she developed in those years was with a local attorney named Joseph A. Jordan Jr. She had no idea in 1955 that eleven years later he would represent her before the U.S. Supreme Court in her own landmark case. Mr. Jordan was born in Norfolk a year before Mama.

His father was a baker and his mother had been a teacher, but she gave up working to raise their children. He graduated from Booker T. Washington High School in 1939, and went to junior college at the Norfolk branch of Virginia Union, which later became Norfolk State University, an institution catering mostly to black students. At the beginning of World War II, he and several of his classmates volunteered for the Army Reserve. They were called up and made part of the infantry. Mr. Jordan told historian Tommy Bogger in 1989 that none of the students, who were the cream of young black men from such colleges as Lincoln, Union, Howard and Morgan, were recruited into the Army Air Corps, though they'd wanted that assignment and to be given a shot at becoming officers. His outfit was sent to the European theater and eventually became part of a quartermaster unit transporting gasoline to the front. Mr. Jordan was trained as a second-echelon mechanic. Two months after D-Day, his unit crossed the English Channel. "There were still bodies floating in the water," he told Bogger, "but we were fortunate we did not have to fight our way through the beaches. Once there, we were under air attack and everything else."

On a foggy, rainy day in Strasbourg, France, not far from the German border, Mr. Jordan was riding in a Jeep that slid off the road and hit a land mine. There were no known mine fields in the area, and the explosion was unexpected. Mr. Jordan was transported to Paris, then to McGuire Army Hospital in Richmond, Virginia, where he was in rehabilitation until 1949. He had come home, but as a paraplegic.

He learned to use a wheelchair, married his college sweetheart, Patricia Gardner, and completed his degree at Virginia Union. Because no law schools in Virginia admitted blacks, he and his bride moved to New York City, where he attended Brooklyn Law School. He completed his degree in 1952 and returned to Virginia to take the bar exam. He began his law career with a classmate from Virginia Union, J. Hugo Madison, who worked with the NAACP. He was twenty-nine years old.

Mr. Jordan's legal practice did not make him rich. He represented clients who were poor and couldn't offer much for his services. His wife Patricia worked as a librarian in the Norfolk school system, and her support enabled him to take up civil rights law. He was not able to come into our house because of his wheelchair. I remember hearing his name before I met him. I think my mother felt somewhat protective of him because, like my father, he was a disabled veteran. Those who assumed a birth defect had put him in his wheelchair received a swift correction from Mama.

It was her great fortune to have a group of friends in the 1950s who were not afraid to challenge the system. They picketed, organized voter registration drives, campaigned for candidates, wrote letters, attended meetings, and they filed lawsuits. I remember these adults through a child's eye, and it seemed to me that my mother and her friends had a great deal of fun working in the fight for civil rights. I look at the photos of my mother and the other women working in Mr. Jordan's cramped office, and there is always someone with a look of pure joy in the picture. At the NAACP, some of her friends included Alice and Melvin Green, Marie Young, John Golden, Dr. Samuel Coppage, Vivian Carter Mason, Annie Nickens, Alveta and Walter Green, Agnes Jordan, Louberta Woody, George Banks, William Tally, Victor Ashe, Len Holt, Edward Dawley, Jr., James Jones, Rev. W.L. Hamilton, Rev. W. L. Hildebrand, and Rev. Thomas

Venable. The Norfolk NAACP had a membership of around three thousand people, so I could not possibly list them all, but I know my mother's success as an activist depended on a great many people in the community.

The Brown decision was handed down on Monday, May 17, 1954, but the story did not run in Norfolk's black newspaper until Saturday, May 22—which just happened to be my mother's thirtieth birthday. A double-deck headline across the front page of the *Journal and Guide* announced, "Court Calls For Fall Hearings To Work Out Plan For School Integration." The lead article cautioned readers: "Pupils Will Not Be Mixed Right Away." Accompanying the articles was a photo of seven attorneys who had worked on the case, and the caption anonymously credited over sixty lawyers, historians and social scientists who had compiled the massive document the plaintiffs had presented to the Court. Six of the seven attorneys in the photo were black, a point of pride in our community. Oliver Hill and Spottswood Robinson III handled the Virginia case. Thurgood Marshall, head of the NAACP legal staff, argued the South Carolina case. The other three black attorneys were Robert Carter, George Hayes and James Nabrit. The one white plaintiffs' attorney, Jack Greenberg, pressed the Delaware case. In all, there were twenty-one states that had traditionally segregated their public schools, and they weren't restricted to the Deep South: The practice had taken root in the Midwest, the Southwest, and even in Wyoming.

The cases had been argued in December 1952. The justices were divided on a constitutional issue: Did the Fourteenth Amendment guaranteeing equal protection of the law specifically prohibit segregated schools? Schools for black children in

Kansas were not held to be substantially different from, or inferior to, those attended by white children, and the state government there was in the process of eliminating mandatory school segregation even before oral arguments began. That wasn't the only quirk in the case. Justice Hugo Black, an Alabaman who had once belonged to the Ku Klux Klan, was an ardent opponent of school segregation because he believed it violated the Fourteenth Amendment.

I don't intend to relitigate the case here, but I do want to devote just a few words to the path the court took to its decision. In brief, the court was split, and Chief Justice Fred Vinson worried that a divided opinion on such an important question would do more harm than good. So, the justices instructed both sides in the case to return the following term after researching the Amendment's history, and to be ready to answer some questions. Namely, what was the original intent of the Congress framing the Amendment? Did it intend for it to specifically prohibit separate schools? How had school segregation come to be, and how had it become so widespread?

A second round of oral arguments was set for October 1953. Then, in September, Chief Justice Fred Vinson suffered a fatal heart attack at the age of sixty-three. A former Governor of California, Earl Warren, was appointed to replace him, and the cases were reargued in December 1953, when Warren had been on the high court for only two months.

Spottswood Robinson argued on behalf of the plaintiffs that the Amendment's intent was to establish legal equality of all persons, regardless of race, and to prohibit any racial caste system. Therefore, school segregation was naturally prohibited. John W. Davis argued on behalf of the defendants that after passage of the Fourteenth Amendment, Congress passed a Freedman's Bureau bill that gave it the power to buy sites and build schools for freedmen and their children. Congress also passed a second act dealing with distribution of funds between schools for black and white children. He inferred from these two bills that the framers of the Fourteenth Amendment never intended for it to outlaw segregated schools.

An Assistant U.S. Attorney General, J. Lee Rankin, told the court that the government had approached the historical question as a historian would, without trying to argue for either side. Its analysis concluded that the topic of educating newly freed Negroes was very much discussed during the Amendment's genesis, but not within the context of the Amendment itself. Public education had not been widespread at the time; schooling was primarily private, and the historical record on the framers' original intent was thus inconclusive. That said, the position of the Department of Justice on the Amendment's meaning was clear—it forbade discrimination based on race in any facet of American life, including public education. Thurgood Marshall, lead counsel for the NAACP, suggested that the question before the court was whether the customs and mores of states like South Carolina and Virginia would prevail over the avowed intent of the Constitution.

Paul Wilson gave the court a history lesson on Kansas' proud abolitionist tradition. He pointed out that Kansas was financed and settled by the Immigrant Aid Society of Boston. Its Free Soil Party was an offshoot of an East Coast abolitionist group. He claimed that Kansas contributed more troops to the Union Army, as a percentage of its population, than any other state. The Kansas legislature of 1867 was comprised almost entirely of former Union soldiers who had risked their lives to free the slaves. That legislative body ratified the Fourteenth Amendment, and six weeks later passed legislation providing for separate educational facilities for black and white children. The Kansas experience seemed to raise more questions among the Justices than it answered. Did the state's history simply demonstrate that prejudice was stronger than principle?

Chief Justice Warren brokered a unanimous decision for the plaintiffs in Brown. "In approaching this problem," he wrote for the court, "we cannot turn the clock back to 1868, when the Amendment was adopted, or even to 1896, when *Plessy v. Ferguson* was written. We must consider public education in light of its full development and its present place in American life throughout the Nation. Only in this way can it be determined if segregation in public schools deprives these plaintiffs of the equal protection of the laws." All nine Justices agreed that it did.

The court recognized that education was a local issue and differed across the country. It did not hand down instructions for the implementation of desegregation. Instead, it asked the parties to return in the fall to answer three questions. First, whether colored children should be immediately admitted to a school of their choice within normal geographic school districts. Second, whether the court should permit an effective, gradual transition. And third, whether the Supreme Court should itself enter a detailed decree, or remand the cases to the lower courts to enter decrees.

Norfolk community leaders were publicly optimistic, based on the segregation of its neighborhoods, that things would not change much. "Here we are pretty well districted," Schools Superintendent J.J. Brewbaker was quoted as saying in the *Journal and Guide*, "and few schools would have both negro and white students. Schools are located so that many will go on as they have been. Our main concern is that (the decision) be looked at calmly, and without emotion, and that we don't let our feelings get in the way."

School Board Chairman J. Farley Power agreed. "The [neighborhood] lines are pretty well drawn here," he said. "All the schools are full and I don't see where there will be much shifting. This is the time to be cool, calm and collected. It is no time for hysteria."

Lucius Robertson, principal of the all-black John Goode and Stonewall Jackson schools, was also quoted in the newspaper, predicting the decision would bring no violence to the city. Principal Winston Douglas of Booker T. Washington High School, agreed: "Elementary schools are situated as to serve an area almost completely one thing or another. Residential patterns will operate. I don't look forward, in a place like Norfolk, to any great disturbance."

In Richmond, Governor Thomas B. Stanley appeared to be supportive of the court's edict, at least at first. He planned, he said, to call public officials together to find a solution that was acceptable to both citizens and the Supreme Court.

Even as a child, I knew Brown was something big and it would directly affect me. I might go to Norview instead of Oakwood. But not right away. My mother was skeptical of the confident sentiments expressed in the newspaper. She heard the reaction of U.S. Senator Harry F. Byrd loudly and clearly when he issued a statement calling the Brown decision "the most serious blow that has yet been struck against the rights of the states in a matter vitally affecting their authority and welfare.

"The decision will be deplored by millions of Americans," Byrd said, "and, instead of promoting the education of our children, it is my belief that it will have the opposite effect in many areas of the country. In Virginia, we are facing now a crisis of the first magnitude."

Mama knew the senator spoke for a powerful majority in the state, and that there was going to be a fight. Byrd had been involved in Virginia politics since 1915, when he was elected state senator, and later had led the Democratic State Central Committee. His political philosophy favored laissez-faire economics, small and debt-free government, and state's rights. He served one term as governor, during which he downsized the state's administration. In 1933, he was appointed to replace a U.S. senator who'd been named secretary of the navy, and he still held the seat. His vast and influential political network was called the Byrd Organization, and among his critics was known as the Byrd Machine.

How much of a stranglehold did he have on Virginia politics? A 1949 study by V.O. Key, Southern Politics in State and Nation, described Virginia as an oligarchy because political power was concentrated in the hands of so few. Through poll taxes and other regulations, only 10 or 12 percent of adults cast votes, meaning the Byrd Organization needed only 5 to 7 percent of the voting-age population to win elections. Key wryly commented, "By contrast, Mississippi is a hotbed of democracy."

State legislatures in Georgia, South Carolina and Mississippi stated they would convert the public schools to private schools rather than integrate. Virginia was reported to be considering the same option. Governor Talmadge of Georgia even signaled that he would call out the militia to prevent integration. Nothing was scheduled to happen right away, however.

Our attention in the summer of 1954 was fastened on a nearby neighborhood called Coronado. It was a white community of about three hundred homes occupied by middle-income families whose children attended white elementary, junior high and high schools. Because many of its residents were military, turnover was high. Naturally, middle-class black families wanted to move to Coronado, because its homes were nicer than those in the black neighborhoods next door—Oakwood, Lincoln Park and Rosemont, where a single block might contain both well-built homes and tarpaper shacks. The dividing line between Coronado and its black neighbors was Widgeon Road, used by both whites and blacks.

North of Coronado, new black developments with 871 housing units had been under construction since 1950, but there was still a shortage of housing for middle-class black families. Mamie Homes, Chesapeake Manor Apartments and Chesapeake Gardens simply did not contain enough to meet demand. One day, a black couple looked at a house on the north side of Widgeon Road. A navy housewife walked across the road and asked if they would like to see her house. They did—and paid a higher price for it than the seller would have asked of a white family. With that, other navy families began selling to black families. The reaction was swift. Whites began driving around Coronado in caravans, even whites who did not live there, to intimidate potential black buyers. A sign, reading, "No nigers wanted" [sic], appeared. Bricks and bottles were hurled at houses. Pipes were ripped out of one home, flooding it a day before its new occupants were to move in. Another was set on fire, and a third was splattered with paint. Finally, a bomb was thrown at a house and automobile. County officials were eager to downplay the violence. An officer suggested to reporters that the bomb crater might have been dug by a dog burying a bone. At a neighborhood meeting, white activists from the community proposed forming a corporation with a covenant that all homes in Coronado be sold only to whites. They offered the services of a white realtor to relocate new black residents to other neighborhoods. Attorney J. Hugo Madison, representing several black families at the meeting, rejected the "sell out and get out" plan. Instead, a neighborhood organization was formed, the Tidewater Civic League. The group held two meetings with the sheriff and the commonwealth's attorney. "When the Negroes moved into Coronado," the sheriff told the members, "they knew they were not wanted by the white residents of that section, and they knew they would have trouble trying to live there."

The Brown case was back in the news in the closing days of August. Governor Thomas B. Stanley had appointed a commission of state senators, all white and all male, to make recommendations as to how Virginia should deal with the Supreme Court directive to integrate the schools. Commonly called the Gray Commission—after its chairman, Senator Garland Gray— it comprised, in large part, members from rural districts whose constituents vehemently opposed the ruling. Ominously, no black community leaders or educators were asked to participate.

Then, on a Sunday evening four days later, a dynamite bomb demolished the front of a house in Coronado while the couple who owned it sat just a few feet away in the kitchen. The publisher of the *Journal and Guide*, P.B. Young, forwarded photos of the bomb damage to the Federal Bureau of Investigation, and sent a telegram to the governor requesting that he intervene. After yet another blast, the Tidewater Civic League sent a lengthy telegram to the governor, too. "We beg you to intervene immediately and order state police to restore law and order," it read, "so that law abiding citizens of Virginia may live peaceably in their homes." A round-the-clock patrol by county and state police began almost immediately.

Even so, one night three bullets were fired into the new home of a mailman and his wife. The bullets lodged in the walls and the couple escaped harm. The head of the local NAACP, Robert D. Robertson, received death threats by phone, and a prankster called a local funeral home to report that Robertson was dead. When a hearse pulled up outside a short while later, Robertson called the funeral director to report that he was still alive. Fourteen black families had bought homes in Coronado, and another twenty waited to close on their purchases. The violence did not stop them from moving in. Eventually, all of the neighborhood's white families sold their homes. The white banking establishment stopped financing white purchasers in Coronado, and even the Veteran's Administration began lowering the value of home appraisals as the neighborhood transitioned from white to black.

In September, while Coronado was in turmoil, my mother walked with me to Miss Alberta's kindergarten each morning and picked me up each afternoon. Young though I was, I knew of the bombings. Mama did not dwell on the violence, but as always, she told me not to talk to strangers. She assured me that our house was safe, that no one driving by would bomb it.

The old combined elementary and high school that my mother and her siblings had attended had been closed since the early 1950s. My sister Jeanette was attending the new Oakwood Elementary in our neighborhood. It was close enough to our house that my mother allowed Jeanette to walk to school with her friends. My oldest sister, Patricia, paid to ride the city bus to St. Joseph's, a black Catholic school, because the year before she had been bused to school in Chesapeake, a suburb fifteen miles away.

The county had provided a rickety old bus to transport black high schoolers to Chesapeake. Sometimes it broke down and the students would be stranded, waiting for another bus to pick them up. Communications were not what they are today: When children did not come home on time, parents would be left wondering whether there had been an accident, and whether their children were safe. In the winter, my sister waited for the bus in the dark. I don't know at what point my mother had had enough, but she told my father they were going to come up with tuition money to send Patricia to Catholic school closer to home.

Meanwhile, the resistance to Brown continued to take shape. A new citizens' group calling itself the Defenders of State Sovereignty and Individual Liberties was created to preserve strict racial segregation in Virginia's schools. The group saw itself as an advocacy organization for white people, a counterpart to the NAACP. They began working on a 7,500-word strategy for fighting the federal order to desegregate. They also recruited like-minded parents and eventually grew into an influential statewide organization with twelve thousand members.

On January 1, 1955, Norfolk officially annexed Tanner's Creek, a vast swath of territory east of the city. It included the black neighborhoods of Oakwood, Rosemont, Chesapeake Gardens, Chesapeake Manor, and Mamie Homes, the transitioning neighborhood Coronado, and the white neighborhoods of Norview and Broad Creek. It also included Broad Creek Navy Housing, and large tracts of open land slated for development to alleviate Norfolk's housing shortage, especially in the black community.

Shortly after annexation, the *Journal and Guide* published an article, with pictures, of the worst housing in the area, and containing the promise that higher taxes would translate into better living. The focus was on areas of Oakwood and Rosemont that could only be described as shantytowns. Since before the turn of the century, poor blacks had been able to buy cheap pieces of land on the outskirts of white settlements, and throw together houses made of scrap lumber and tarpaper. Few had toilets or running water. Renovating these tumbledown shacks was not feasible. They seemed destined for demolition.

My mother worried about the future of people who lived in those shanties, and in homes like ours as well. Our street was certainly not a shantytown. Its shotgun houses, like ours, were small but comfortable, even if they did rely on outhouses in their back yards. My friend Maxine lived next door in a larger clapboard house that boasted a dining room. Mr. Herbert Smith, a mason, had built a brick house two doors down on the corner. Most people in our neighborhood had their own vegetable garden. My sister Jeanette had fond memories of the days when we had an icebox in the kitchen and a man with a horse and buggy delivered ice every day. After annexation, horses were not allowed in Oakwood, and another vendor who delivered by horse-drawn cart—my grandfather's friend Mr. Goldie Brown—was forced to find someone to take his horses. He had a fairly large piece of land where he grew collard greens, butter beans, peas and other vegetables, and made his living selling the produce, which he then delivered. I can only imagine that he was devastated when annexation upended his way of life.

I don't remember the ice man, but I do remember the ice cream man. He came by in a truck every afternoon. I would run back to my Granddaddy's little house and beg him for a popsicle. He would say, "Weenie, I don't have any money." Then he would wait until the last second before giving me a nickel. Granddaddy planted a big vegetable garden out back and flowers in front. He grew rose bushes and sunflowers on the east side of the house and he used to chase my friends out of the yard so they wouldn't run over his flowers.

One Easter, my mother gave us a box of chicks to raise. All of them died except for one rooster. He terrorized us whenever we went in the back yard, so my cousin Howard drove him to his father's farm, about fifty miles away. We had strong family ties to our neighborhood, and my mother was determined to protect it, no matter how poor it looked to outsiders.

After annexation, both of my sisters had to pay to ride the bus to Norfolk schools. Transportation was not free. My sister Patricia was able to attend Booker T. Washington High School instead of St. Joe's, now that we were part of the city. The Supreme Court delivered its second decision in the Brown case in May 1955, leaving the matter of how to desegregate schools up to the states, famously directing them to act "with all deliberate speed."

I started first grade at Oakwood Elementary that fall. Once again, my mother sewed a new plaid dress for me to wear on the first day of school. She walked with me every morning and picked me up in the afternoon. Children who lived in Rosemont had to walk much farther to Oakwood, as there was no bus to take them to school. My teacher in first grade—and in second and third, as well—was Miss Eileen Lee. I loved her. She was single and lived in downtown Norfolk. A few of our teachers lived in the county, but many drove out of the city to teach us. All of the elementary school's teachers were women; the only men in the building were the janitor and the principal, Mr. Hughes. Oakwood Elementary was the center of our community. Many mothers participated in the PTA. My mother knew all the teachers and took an active interest in my schooling. On special occasions or holidays, she would be a "room mother" and help the teacher with any special festivities.

In November 1955, the Gray Commission dropped the first bombshell announcing how Virginia would deal with Brown. Echoing Senator Byrd's immediate reaction to school desegregation, the commission decided after fourteen months of meetings that the Supreme Court was practicing "judicial legislation" that threatened "the fundamental. . . rights of the states." In a nod to the Defenders of State Sovereignty and Individual Liberties, its report accused the Court of giving "no consideration to the adverse effect of integration upon white children." It praised Virginia's existing school system and concluded that segregation was best for both races. The commission recommended amending Section 141 of the Virginia State Constitution, which prohibited spending public funds on private education. It favored allowing local school boards to close public schools rather than integrate, while providing tuition grants for parents who wanted to send their children to private academies. Localities that wanted to integrate would have the power to assign pupils to schools in order to manage integration. Of all the state's major newspapers, only Norfolk's *The Virginian-Pilot* opposed the plan.

The Byrd Organization was not satisfied. It opposed the local option proposed by the Gray Commission. Nothing but total refusal to cooperate with the federal government would be tolerated in Virginia. Governor Stanley reversed his initial calm reaction to Brown, and asked the General Assembly to convene a special session. He requested a referendum so that voters could amend the constitution to allow tuition grants to private institutions. The legislature was busy with its own dark machinations: On February 1, 1956, it adopted a Resolution of Interposition, which claimed that state sovereignty trumped decisions by the federal government, and that Virginia was thus not bound by edicts from Washington.

On February 24, 1956, Senator Byrd introduced a phrase into our lives that would dominate the school integration issue for the foreseeable future. He officially kicked off "Massive Resistance" to school integration. On March 12, he created the Southern Manifesto, signed by 101 Southern members of Congress, which called for opposition to Brown. Voters in Virginia amended the state constitution to allow for tuition grants. The fight was on.

While all of this was occurring, Mama and her friends were still meeting to come up with a strategy to prevent our neighborhood from being slated for redevelopment and bulldozed. Thankfully, the *Journal and Guide* realized that many of the homes in the annexed area were well-built and well-maintained. It published a February 1956 article featuring photos of homes in Oakwood, Lincoln Park and Rosemont, and arguing that their values would increase if the streets were paved, drainage was improved, sidewalks were installed, and the city provided such services as water and sewage.

Later that year, when the city unveiled a plan to redevelop those neighborhoods, it did not go as anticipated. A special "Land Committee" proposed a massive reclamation project in a 370-acre area of one thousand existing homes. It would have replaced the structures with 2,500 units, among them single-family houses, apartments and duplexes. Like the NHRA Project One, the plan included playgrounds, an elementary school and a shopping center. My mother was not on board with the idea, because she knew most residents were too poor to buy the new homes—they were just scraping by, as it was. One elderly resident told *The Virginian-Pilot*, "We old people can't buy new homes. If you take our homes, we'll just be out in the street." As had been the case in Coronado, residents realized they had to organize to have a voice in the future of their neighborhoods.

I believe that this is when my mother became president of the Oakwood and Rosemont Civic League. It had about thirty members, including my mother's friends Alice and Melvin Green, Herbert Smith, Annie Nickens, Norman Cofer and my kindergarten teacher, Alberta Smith. The threat of redevelopment made her intensely political. I remember my Aunt Pudney complaining, "When she calls me on the phone, it's all about politics, all the time! I don't want to hear it anymore."

Community meetings at Mt. Gilead Baptist or Oakwood Chapel Church became urgent. Everyone realized the residents needed legal help to stop or alter the redevelopment plan. Attorneys Joe Jordan and J. Hugo Madison were the most active in advocating for the successful preservation of Oakwood. Amazingly, the Oakwood redevelopment plans were tabled due to public opposition. My mother and her colleagues were unwilling to do things the old way, and go along with the plans of so-called experts. They were younger and bolder than the conservative business leaders who came before them.

Simultaneously, in May 1956, attorney Victor Ashe of the NAACP filed a lawsuit in federal court to force the integration of Norfolk's public schools. It had been a year since *Brown II* ordered states to implement desegregation with "all deliberate speed." Instead, Virginia had pushed back with Massive Resistance forcing the black community to push forward with massive activism. A similar lawsuit was filed in Newport News.

Sixty-five students and thirty-one parents were part of the lawsuit styled *Leola Beckett v. School Board of the City of Norfolk*, because Beckett was the first of the plaintiffs' names, alphabetically. The suit was filed in U.S. District Court for the Eastern District of Virginia, in the courtroom of Judge Walter "Beef" Hoffman. He was a Republican, newly appointed by President Eisenhower, and had deep roots in Norfolk and friends in both political parties. One of the first decisions he handed down required the desegregation of Seashore State Park in Virginia Beach. Rather than comply, the governor closed the beach, and it would remain closed until 1963.

On August 27, 1956, the governor called the General Assembly into special session to pass "The Stanley Plan," which established a three-member, governor-appointed Pupil Placement Board to determine where students would attend school.

It also authorized him to close any integrated public school in the state, regardless of the wishes of the local school board. Clearly, the Pupil Placement Board existed to prevent integration, not facilitate it. The Stanley Plan was exactly what the Defenders and the Byrd Machine wanted.

Judge Hoffman declared the Pupil Placement Act unconstitutional, and the Norfolk and Newport News plaintiffs won their first round in federal court. It was the first of several NAACP victories. By the fall, area parks, recreation centers, and transportation facilities were ordered by a federal judge to desegregate or shut down.

But at the same time, redevelopment of Norfolk's neighborhoods was rolling out in such a way that racially segregated neighborhoods were preserved, which inevitably would lead to segregated schools. New school construction sites were carefully selected to further ensure that few black children would be eligible to attend white schools. Mayor W. Fred Duckworth was both accused of and credited with practicing "bulldozer diplomacy," because he was literally demolishing neighborhoods and building new schools to sidestep integration.

Judge Hoffman ordered Norfolk's School Board to abolish the practice of assigning students to schools based on race by August 1957. The superintendent of Norfolk's schools appealed the decision, asking for more time before "attempting to mix the children." Though Judge Hoffman expressed his annoyance with the board's refusal to comply with the ruling, the appeal stalled any action for another school year. Finally, in June 1958, Hoffman issued a supplemental directive to integrate. Norfolk's superintendent had no choice but to start accepting applications from black students who wanted to transfer to white schools.

I had just finished third grade at Oakwood. For the coming year, Mama told me she was going to apply to send me to Norview Elementary School, the white school close to our house.

CHAPTER FOUR

KICKING UP A FUSS

For four years, I had heard Mama talk about school desegregation at home, in public, on the phone. Sometimes she dragged me to meetings if she couldn't find a babysitter. I knew how important it was to her that I gain admission to a white school. I wasn't apprehensive about attending one, though I loved going to school at Oakwood.

Norview schools were near our neighborhood—I could see them from the bus window on rides downtown—but I had never even walked across the grounds. Oakwood Elementary was a new school and it looked similar to Norview Elementary. The county might have used the same architectural plans for both. I didn't know any of the children who went to Norview, as I don't think I knew any white children at all, and I knew that if I told Mama I did not want to go to Norview, she'd probably let me stay at Oakwood.

But by mid-July, 151 applications had been submitted, and mine was one of them. My mother attended a school board meeting where she and the other parents and guardians received a memo informing them that psychological tests would be administered to the students who had applied to transfer. Parents were directed to accompany their applicant children to the Office of Psychological Services at the John Marshall School in downtown Norfolk. We were told to bring a lunch, because one would not be provided.

Parents were insulted that their children would be tested in order to transfer. There were academic tests in addition to the psychological interview. The NAACP sponsored a meeting that filled the large Mt. Gilead Baptist Church, just down the street from our house. Robert D. Robertson, the organization's president, listened to the parents complain that if black and white schools were supposedly equal, why would black children need to be tested when white children were not? Mr. Robertson, and the NAACP in general, were somewhat conservative in their approach to handling racial progress. Mr. Robertson was a union organizer, so negotiating with powerful interests was his life's work. He was schooled in the art of compromise. Ironically, many white folks thought the NAACP was radical, especially Norfolk's Mayor Duckworth. The General Assembly had investigated the NAACP's activities and subpoenaed its members, which they'd viewed as an attempt at intimidation.

Mr. Robertson encouraged the parents to go along with the school board's plans. Some of the parents felt that the community should fight back against the testing requirement. Some parents simply refused to allow their children to be tested, especially to submit to the psychological testing. In this instance, my mother backed up Robertson. We were in the front pew. She stood and faced the audience behind us, saying, "I'm insulted too. But I'm going to take Charlene for that testing. It's already the middle of the summer. If we fight this, it will only delay getting the children into school. We've got our foot in the door and we should move forward."

I was accustomed to my mother voicing her opinion. She had a loud voice and she always spoke with confidence. I was proud to be her daughter. Of the 151 student applicants, 63 declined to either take the test or be interviewed and they were denied the opportunity to transfer.

I was scheduled to appear for testing at the John Marshall school at 9 a.m. on July 31, which meant we had to get on the bus at about eight o'clock. My mother was often late for meetings, partly because we didn't have a car and she was always looking for a ride. But that morning, we made sure we were early. The school was located at Fifteenth and Omohundro streets in East Ghent, a neighborhood I'd never visited. When it was built during the Gilded Age, East Ghent was an affluent neighborhood with a European flavor about it, with grand houses and lovely apartments lining tree-lined boulevards. By 1958, East Ghent had lost some of its luster. The houses were not slums, by any means, but many had been divided into apartments. The school was a massive brick building, old but well-maintained.

We walked up a long staircase to the front doors. Someone at a desk in the lobby told us which room I should report to for testing. Because the testing was done on a weekday, some parents had to take off from work to be there. I think there were about ten other children in the room with me. I don't remember buildings being air-conditioned in the 1950s, so I will assume there was a fan. Whatever the case, the room was hot. Our parents were interviewed while we took the test.

A woman passed out answer sheets for a California standardized achievement test. I had taken a test almost exactly like it in third grade. The test was long. I can't remember exactly how many hours we sat there, but it took up the whole morning and then we ate our lunches in the cafeteria with our parents.

In the afternoon, I had my psychological evaluation. Mama was in the room with me. The only thing my mother told me beforehand was to speak clearly, loudly, and without fear. I think there were five white people, two men and three women, including Superintendent Brewbaker. It wasn't a long conversation. They asked my mother why I wanted to go to Norview instead of Oakwood. She told them it was closer. They asked how much closer, and she told them about four blocks. They asked if I would have to cross a highway to walk to Norview. She assured them that I could walk on a dirt path where no cars could drive. They asked us both how we would feel if I was the only black student in the class. Would I feel at home? I answered, "When I get to know the children better, I can make friends." Mr. Brewbaker asked me, "Have you played with white children?" I told him I had, at a house where my mother worked. My mother added that I was in Girl Scouts, and played with white children in Coronado. As usual, I was wearing a dress my mother had made for me. It was sleeveless. I don't remember what my mother wore, but I'm sure she was dressed up, too. When it was over, we walked out into the humid, blast-furnace heat. There wasn't any place to buy a soda or ice cream near the school, so we just walked to the bus stop. Mama told me she was proud of me.

To our great dismay, the school board passed a resolution in August denying transfers to all 151 students. The resolution said that the board "believes that the individual applicants would receive no educational benefit from the requested assignment, but would only suffer thereby. It is believed that the isolation which would be caused by such an assignment would be detrimental to educational progress and may well cause emotional instability and even be detrimental to health."

I was one of eight Oakwood Elementary students who'd applied, along with Glenda Brothers, Melvin Green, Minnie Green, Cloroteen Harris, Rosa Mae Harris, Sherron Smith, and Edward Smith. We were denied transfer because a new school, Rosemont Elementary, was slated to open in our neighborhood in 1959, and the board did not want to transfer us twice. The board also worried that it was "not in the best interest of the applicants nor of the present students to grant such petitions," because "Racial conflicts have occurred in this area in the past and the Board is of the opinion that integration there would renew such conflicts and produce grave administration problems within the second system—all to the detriment of good education and the public welfare." The board was referring to Coronado, and it wasn't entirely wrong. There had been a cross burning on Johnston Road in Chesapeake Gardens, near the home of one of the students who had applied to go to Norview.

Even as the board was denying the 151 applications, hearings in the Beckett case were being held in Judge Hoffman's courtroom. Apparently, the school board never informed Judge Hoffman of its intention to test the transfer students: He'd learned of it while reading the newspaper. Some parents who objected to the testing had filed a motion requesting students be admitted without it. The school board wanted to delay admission of the transfer students until the 1959 school year. My mother and

I rode the bus downtown to watch the hearings every day. These were the dog days of August, hot and sweaty and humid. Federal court was near the corner of Granby Street and Brambleton Avenue, in the same massive limestone building as the main post office—an Art Deco monument to the permanence, gravity and might of the federal government, with marble steps, high ceilings, and brass elevators. It was the most impressive building I'd ever seen. I was bored out of my mind in court, but I liked being in that building.

One day, I was playing in our front yard when I noticed a car parked in front of our house, a white man behind the wheel. He seemed out of place in our neighborhood, and with a second, closer look I recognized him from the courtroom. I ran into the house and shouted to Mama, "The man from court is in front of our house!" She came to the front door and peered outside. "That's J.J. Brewbaker, superintendent of schools," she said. Mama rushed back into the house and called attorneys Victor Ashe and Hugo Madison. They thought Brewbaker was likely measuring the distance from our house to Oakwood Elementary to prove that it was closer than Norview.

On August 25, the Norfolk School Board submitted a statement into evidence from Brewbaker. The exhibit contained the mileage between Oakwood and Rosemont schools from the homes of the eight pupils who had applied to go to Norview Elementary. Attorney Joe Jordan called Alice Green, Fannie Harris and Mama as witnesses. He asked each of the witnesses about the distance they lived from Oakwood Elementary and Norview Elementary. Mama testified that we lived five blocks from Norview and approximately eleven blocks from Oakwood. I had to cross Sewell's Point Road, a two-lane highway, to get to

Oakwood, but I could walk to Norview on a path at the end of our street on which cars did not drive. The School Board attorney cross-examined her about the distance to Oakwood. It was a repeat of the questions I was asked during my psychological evaluation.

"When you say approximately, what does that mean?

"Well, I measured them myself, so some blocks have—well, some are a little longer than others, so I measured about eleven blocks."

"Do you mean that there are eleven blocks, some of them short and some of them long?"

"Yes, sir."

"And that there are five blocks from your home to Norview?"

"Yes, sir."

"And those blocks must be long blocks, mustn't they?"

She explained the route that I would walk to Norview. He questioned her ability to calculate the distance from our house because an automobile could not drive on the route where I would walk.

"Why are you sure that you do not live just about the same distance from Norview that you live from Oakwood? Isn't it just about the same?"

"Well, I have measured it by the blocks, and that's all I can go by."

As far as I know, this was the first time my mother had ever testified in court. I was sitting in the front row, behind Mr. Ashe, who sat at the plaintiff's table. It was pretty cool to watch my mother testify. But, I could tell by her facial expression that she was peeved at the attorney who cross-examined her—he asked his questions as though he was questioning her intelligence or honesty. When we got home, she chuckled at Brewbaker coming all the way out to our house to measure the distance to Norview, but getting it wrong. Of course, I would walk the shortest distance, and not take a route that a car would drive. There was a time when black people could not testify against white people. It was gratifying to watch Judge Hoffman interact with the school board attorneys. He made the defense attorneys squirm.

On the same day my mother testified, August 29, the Norfolk School Board gave Judge Hoffman a list of seventeen students who could transfer to white junior and senior high schools. They had a legal right rising out of the fact that their homes were indisputably closer to a white school than a black one. Their names were Geraldine Talley, Louis Cousins, Betty Jean Reed, Lolita Portis, Reginald Young, LaVera Forbes, James Turner, Jr., Patricia Turner, Edward Jordan, Claudia Wellington, Andrew Heidelberg, Alvarez Frederick Gonsouland, Delores Johnson, Johnnie Rouse, Olivia Driver, Carol Wellington, and Patricia Godbolt. They would come to be known as the Norfolk Seventeen.

The School Board members were faced with the prospect of going to federal prison if they defied Judge Hoffman's order. They met at the bedside of board member Francis Crenshaw who had just undergone an emergency appendectomy. Their consensus was that integration might be easier to accept if the local school board made the decision, instead of having it forced upon the community by a federal court. They could not have been more wrong. The board was vilified. The Byrd Machine, and newly elected Governor J. Lindsay Almond, viewed the decision as betrayal. Instead of obeying the Massive Resistance laws of Virginia and supporting the doctrine of interposition, the board chose to follow the dictates of the federal government. School opening was delayed for two weeks to allow time to prepare for integration of the seventeen black students into six of the city's all-white junior high and high schools, where 9,930 white children were enrolled.

Less than a month later, Governor Almond ordered those six schools closed. The doors were padlocked on September 22, 1958. All the black schools and the remaining segregated white schools remained open. At a city council meeting on September 30th, a crowd of 150 people opposed to the school closings packed the council's chambers. They demanded the schools be reopened. Numerous ministers made impassioned pleas on moral grounds, with one stating that American democracy depended on public schools. Mayor Duckworth blurted out, "The best thing you preachers can do is to tell those seventeen niggers to go back where they belong and we'll open the schools tomorrow." The comment was omitted from the official minutes and not reported in the press but it made a lasting impression in the memories of those in the room.

Dueling lawsuits resulted. White parents who wanted the schools reopened filed *Ruth Pendleton James v. J. Lindsay Almond* in federal court. The governor filed a suit before the Virginia Supreme Court, *Albertis S. Harrison v. Sidney C. Day*, that argued closing the schools was lawful. Before the cases were decided by the courts, parents had no choice but to find alternate schooling for their children for the fall semester.

The Norfolk Seventeen were tutored at Bute Street Baptist Church. NAACP attorneys Madison and Ashe were approached by Hortense Wells, a black supervisor in the school district. She encouraged them to prepare the seventeen for the likely animosity they would face when school reopened. Wells brought on Vivian Mason, a nationally renowned social worker from New York, to head up the makeshift Bute Street school. Mason was educated at the University of Chicago and was running her own public relations firm at that time, and her husband was one of Virginia's first black millionaires. Mason hired an integrated staff to teach a dozen subjects to the students, who were in five different grades. Because the school was located in a church, the teachers included spiritual lessons, prayers, and hymns, in an effort to bolster the students' faith that God was on their side. Mason also schooled the students in the facts of life on the front lines of school desegregation. "When you sought entrance to white schools," she told them, "you left your childhood behind."

Many white parents had been preparing for this test from the moment Massive Resistance had been announced. The state was willing to provide tuition grants to white students who chose private education over integration. Some attended existing private academies. The Norfolk Division of the College of William and Mary tutored children of faculty and staff through its Education Department. Some white students commuted to schools in adjacent counties. An organization called the Tidewater Education Foundation, TEF, supported by the Defenders of State Sovereignty, was poised to educate five thousand students in ad-hoc facilities, including churches. The group saw that plan unravel when a good many churches publicly denounced TEF. The Catholic Church was no surprise—it had previously integrated Norfolk's Catholic schools—but Protestant denominations, among them Presbyterians, Lutherans, Episcopalians, and Methodists—followed suit, refusing to provide facilities to TEF.

None of the city's schoolteachers were willing to teach in TEF facilities, dealing a final blow to the organization's hopes for large-scale segregated private education. Finally, TEF opened the Tidewater Academy at Bayview Baptist Church with only six instructors and fewer than sixty students. Other students attended informal tutoring groups that met in homes, commercial spaces, or churches. Roughly two thousand students received no schooling that fall.

A group called the Norfolk Committee for Public Schools formed to advocate reopening the schools, but it lacked the political clout to sway public opinion or influence the city's leaders. A city referendum that November supported keeping the schools closed by a margin of 12,340 votes to 8,712—but given that the population of Norfolk was 300,000, these low numbers reflect the complacency of the citizens, as well as the efficacy of the poll tax in reducing the number of eligible voters.

Closing those schools that might have been integrated had an embarrassing and apparently unanticipated outcome: Norfolk high schools and junior highs that had historically served whites were now shut down, while those that had always catered to blacks were open and running as normal. Black children were still getting an education. So the Norfolk City Council decided to spread the pain around: In January 1959, it voted to cut off funding for all the city's schools above sixth grade. That was a step too far. A group of one hundred business and media leaders presented a petition in support of opening the schools to the city council and published it in *The Virginian-Pilot*. While the advertisement admitted that the signers would prefer segregated schools, a city without public schools was bad for business—and privately, they worried that the closures threatened the city's relationship with its largest employer, the U.S. Navy.

The two lawsuits were decided on January 19, 1958. The federal District Court sided with parents who wanted to reopen the schools. The Virginia Supreme Court decided against the governor, declaring that closing the schools was unlawful. Norfolk's schools were ordered to reopen on February 2, 1959. Of the ten thousand students who had been locked out in September, only 6,400 returned. Some joined the military, some got married, others got jobs. They became known as the "Lost Class of '59."

National and international media were present for the reopening on February 2, 1959, but the day proved anticlimactic. The public remained as complacent as it had been throughout the entire crisis. The Norfolk Seventeen endured the slings of racism, as had been predicted by the school board. Two students had crosses burned on their lawns, one girl had a knife thrown at her, and others dodged rocks and spit. One was chased by a mob on his walk home from school. A white teacher wore gloves whenever he touched anything two black girls had touched, and another showed films that depicted insulting stereotypes of blacks. One boy was called racial epithets every day until he graduated. Two were refused entrance into the National Honor Society. All of the seventeen would later recall their school experience with sadness and pain.

My own experience of integrating a white school was delayed by Mayor Duckworth's bulldozer diplomacy. While Oakwood was spared from redevelopment, Rosemont was slated to be completely demolished. The new elementary school was hastily finished in the Rosemont neighborhood, which prevented me from going to Norview; in the fall of 1959, I started fifth grade at the new Rosemont Elementary. It was a big step down from

Oakwood, and I was the only student from Oakwood who was assigned to that school. All the other children lived in Rosemont. The school was a modular building with 10 classrooms, one boys' and one girls' bathroom. It had no cafeteria, no library, no gym or multi-purpose room, just ten classrooms and an office for the head teacher—we didn't even have a principal. Mama was livid. She took it personally, saying, "They built that school for Charlene because I applied to send her to Norview!"

A similar modular school was built in Coronado, with demountable classrooms taken from Oakwood Elementary. When Coronado was a white neighborhood, neighborhood children had attended Norview schools. Though the Oakwood PTA protested, and my mother kicked up an especially noisy fuss, the board moved forward with its plans to construct the school, averting court-ordered integration of those one hundred elementary-aged students.

Construction at Rosemont continued throughout the year. When the school opened in the fall of 1960 as Rosemont Elementary and Junior High, it had a gym and a cafeteria and a library and an auditorium. It served first through ninth grades, and I stayed a student there for four years. The first year I was in the school, in sixth grade, Mama noticed that my school books were stamped, "Norview Schools." Once again she was furious, because they had built a brand-new school but given us hand-me-down books. She got a ride downtown to the next school board meeting, taking one of my books with her, and demanded in her loud voice that they buy us new books. Right away, the old books disappeared and we got brand-new books in their place. It was one time I wish she had taken me with her to a meeting. I would love to have heard her call them out. My mother didn't cuss. She didn't have to.

Mama was an active PTA mother, but she was not always able to combine her political activism with her school volunteer work. She recounted a story from my junior high days to Tommy Bogger. "Even our principal at the school was afraid to get involved with the parents, and particularly a parent like me, because he was afraid that it might, I guess, cost him his job or something." She recalled putting up a big cardboard chart in the auditorium with all the parents' names on it. Beside every registered voter, she put a gold star. She thought the chart would encourage other parents to register. She had cleared the display with the principal before putting it up. "And then, all of a sudden, we came there to look and he had taken it down. He said he couldn't keep that up there, and we knew because the superintendent downtown had told him not to let us have it there. And this is how we were encouraging our people to register at the school level."

On July 3, 1963, Mama addressed the Citizens Advisory Committee (CAC) meeting, a bi-racial advisory group set up by the Norfolk City Council to study the city's racial problems and recommend solutions. My mother was one of four speakers to address the panel's twenty-five members on the progress being made, or lack thereof, in eliminating racial discrimination in Norfolk. James Gay, a college student, spoke about ordinances that had been passed in Louisville, Kansas City, San Antonio, Oklahoma City, and Philadelphia barring racial discrimination in public accommodations. He encouraged Norfolk to pass a similar ordinance. James Staton, a teacher at Booker T. Washington High School, and P. B. Young, editor and vice president of the *Journal and Guide*, both said their top priority was eliminating discrimination in public accommodations. Mama, as president of the Oakwood-Rosemont Civic League, placed public school integration at the top of her list, and called for a black person to be appointed to the school board. Someone in the crowd asked her if every race and creed should be represented on the School Board. "There is a race barrier between Negroes and whites," she answered, "not between Catholics, Jews and Baptists." She called for an end to token integration that forced children in Oakwood and Rosemont to ride all the way downtown to Booker T. Washington High School when Norview High was right in our neighborhood. At the next council meeting, attorney Hilary Jones was unanimously appointed as the first black on the Norfolk School Board. My mother and Mr. Jordan were campaigning for Dr. William F. Brazziel, coordinator of education at Norfolk State College. Once again, the decision reflected the difference in thinking between those who were incremental and those who wanted to throw caution to the wind to change the status quo.

In September 1963, students at Booker T. Washington staged a walk-out. Over 2,400 students participated to protest overcrowded classes, paint peeling off the walls, a lack of hot water in the showers and restrooms, poor heating in the classrooms, and dim lighting in the hallways. Student leaders presented a petition to the superintendent. Hundreds carried signs protesting the conditions in their school and the slow pace of school desegregation.

The board approved seventy-three transfers, including only fifty-one of the late applicants. At the next CAC meeting, the group's chairman, Robert Ripley, said he thought the picketing was regrettable. "I personally feel that picketing is an insult to the committee," he said. "I think it's wrong, but it's up to the Negroes if that's what they want."

"I regret very much," my mother's replied, "that the CAC has chosen to use its valuable time to criticize our conduct in the picketing of the Norfolk School Administration. In the first instance, it shows a serious lack of understanding of the Norfolk Negro citizens, and in the second instance it is a waste of time if this is intended to discourage us."

In the spring of 1964, the School Board created a "Statement of Choice of Schools" that carved the district into zones. Some zones comprised only one school, and students in these zones attended that school regardless of race. In zones with two or more schools, students had the opportunity to choose the school they wanted to attend. Obviously, white students in these zones would not choose to attend a black school, so the black schools would remain segregated. Mr. Jordan sent a letter to Superintendent E.L. Lambert. "You insult the intelligence of Norfolk's parents and students," he wrote, "when you suggest that your 'Choice of Schools' scheme will do anything more than create needless confusion, and maintain racial discrimination. It is time to grow up. Put away your administrative knee pants, hula hoops and bob jacks."

"Ending school discrimination is a problem in our City solely because your administration has made it so," he charged. "Send Norfolk's students to the school nearest their homes and let's get on with the real problems of quality education."

The Oakwood-Rosemont Civic League struck back against bulldozer diplomacy in February 1964. Mr. Jordan, as counsel for the League, wrote a letter to Robert Weaver, the first black administrator of the Housing and Home Finance Agency. He alerted HHFA that federal funds were being used to maintain racial segregation in Norfolk's schools, writing: "The worst of our fears are now being realized. A brand new segregated Rosemont Elementary School has been built. A brand new segregated Rosemont Junior High School has been built.

"And a brand new segregated Rosemont High School is planned in the same building," Mr. Jordan reported. "Your agency's urban renewal monies are being used by our local redevelopment authority to help finance all of these facilities." The letter urged the HHFA to withdraw certification of the city's redevelopment efforts, pending a probe and correction of its policy. Copies of the letter were sent to President Lyndon Johnson, Representatives Adam Clayton Powell and Charles Diggs, Attorney General Robert Kennedy, and two FHA administrators.

That summer, my mother was among the Norfolkians selected to meet with Weaver in Washington, D.C., to discuss the misuse of HHFA funds. The experience helped crystalize for her the power of grass-roots advocacy. The Rosemont high school was never built. Weaver would go on to be the first black appointed to a cabinet level position as Secretary of Housing and Urban Development in 1966.

Around the same time, the neighborhood we knew as Rosemont was completely leveled. Some of our friends lost their home and moved away. My mother and the Civic League had saved Oakwood, and more: While I was in high school, the city started paving our streets, installing sidewalks and streetlights, and extending sewer and gas lines to our houses. The long nights of work for such change had prepared Mama well for more prominent roles in her city and state.

FEARLESS

I entered Norview High School in tenth grade in September 1964. It was five years after Norfolk integrated its schools and ten years after Brown. In the 1963-64 school year, 517 black students were approved for transfer to desegregated schools across Norfolk. In the following year, 1,251 students were approved.

I think I was more apprehensive to start classes as a black student in a white high school than I was when I was younger. There were about one hundred black students in a student body of perhaps two thousand. Few black teachers taught there. I made a white friend my sophomore year. Fran was in my science class. She knew a friend of mine, Doris Smith, because their fathers were in the army and they'd gone to school together in France. When we were juniors, I saw her in the hallway and shouted, "Hi Fran!" She said something like, "Oh my God," and ran away. In speech class I decided to talk about George Washington Carver and his experiments with peanuts. Boys in the class laughed at my speech, which was not meant to be funny. For the most part, I was the only black student in most of my classes, and the white kids ignored me. My grades were above average. But I do have more strong negative memories than positive.

Still, it wasn't all bad. I remember every year we put on a talent show. My friends and I, who were all black, performed a dance. In junior high, we had been in a dance group and performed all over the city in competitions. The Norview audience liked us—nobody booed! I went to the homecoming football games. Every year my mother sewed a suit for me and bought me a corsage. My favorite was a heather green suit without lapels that crossed over and buttoned. It was so stylish. One year I went with a boy, but we didn't go to the dance—I had to be home early, because my mother was a little strict when it came to boys. I remember going to the senior prom. I was working at Cavalier Cleaners and had my own money, and I bought a dress with an empire waistline that I'd seen in Seventeen magazine. I could find it neither in Norfolk nor on an expedition to Suffolk, so I had to order it. My mother altered it for me because it was too big in the bodice. She relaxed my curfew for senior prom, which was held in Norview's cafeteria. Black and white students both attended, but there were no interracial couples and no black and white kids dancing together.

One of my fondest memories of high school dates to March 1966. My mother's picture was on the front page of *The Virginian-Pilot* when she and Mr. Jordan won the poll tax case in United States Supreme Court. I took the newspaper to school and showed it to my eleventh-grade government teacher. He was very impressed. I did not show it to my white classmates. We weren't that close. I didn't think they cared.

If I am going to be honest, I have to admit that I missed Rosemont Junior High, and my years learning with black teachers and black students. I could have gone to Booker T. Washington High School if I'd wanted to, but I knew that Norview was where I was supposed to be. High school was too late to start an integrated education, I think. Norfolk should have allowed me to attend Norview Elementary five years earlier. The fact that the school district built a new school to evade integration is a stain on the reputations of the city's leaders from that time.

Integration was not easy or pleasant, but it had to happen. We were acting on principle, not for our own personal comfort. My mother attempted to stay active in PTA while I was at Norview. She attended the meetings. But by the time I was in high school, she was increasingly active in politics with Mr. Jordan. She kept an eye on me and made sure that I was well-adjusted, if not deliriously happy.

Our graduation was held outside on Norview's athletic field. Our family still did not have a car, so my cousin Howard brought my parents. I was the last child at home; by then, my sisters were living in California. There were three dozen black graduates in my class of about 700.

When I walked across the stage to get my diploma, I glanced out at the football bleachers, but I couldn't find my family. There were a lot of people, and we were just part of the crowd, not separate, not segregated, finally equal.

CHAPTER FIVE

EARLY CAMPAIGNS

We have to jump back in time a few years to cover some of my favorite memories of my mother's protesting and agitating with her friends. I believe 1959 was the first year they picketed—or, at least, that's the first year I remember their doing it. But, once they started picketing, they developed a real fondness for it.

Down the street from our house on Sewell's Point Road, the area's main drag, was a large grocery, the Be-Lo Supermarket. Sewell's Point Road brought traffic from Broad Creek up to Little Creek Road, which linked the sprawling Norfolk Naval Base to a large naval amphibious base. It was a well-traveled road. Be-Lo gave customers S&H Green Stamps when they bought groceries, and I loved licking the stamps and sticking them into the coupon books. Filled coupon books could be redeemed for household items—toasters, umbrellas, luggage, all manner of stuff.

Be-Lo had both black and white employees. As was the norm, the black workers were stockers and baggers and got paid a lot less than the white cashiers. The butcher and the manager were white and well-paid, while the janitor was black. Sometimes, a black stocker named Miss Josephine would be asked to jump on the cash register when it got busy, but she was not paid a cashier's wages.

We could walk to Be-Lo from our house, which was a good thing, because my parents did not own a car until after I graduated from high school. When Mama shopped, she would just push the shopping cart home and tell us to run it back to Be-Lo for her. The butcher was very fond of Mama. He'd always call out to her when he saw her in the meat department. She gave him a hard time, in a nice way, when the meat looked like it wasn't as fresh as it should have been.

One day she purchased a baking chicken to make one of my favorite dishes, chicken and home-made dumplings. She steamed or boiled the chicken, but not so much that it fell apart, to make broth, then put the bird in the oven to brown it until it was crispy. She steamed the dumplings on top of the broth and made gravy out of it. On this occasion, she'd finished the cooking and our dinner smelled amazing. She cut a leg open, and was surprised to find what appeared to be a tumor inside. She was so mad, she picked up the pan and walked the chicken back to Be-Lo. She showed it to the butcher and said, "How dare you sell me this diseased chicken!" He apologized profusely and hurried to give her a refund, but now we had no dinner: She left the entire meal at the store, dumplings and all. From that point on, the butcher teased her. "When are you going to bring us some more of your chicken?" he'd ask her. "That was great!"

A few days before Christmas one year, my mother and at least a dozen people decided to picket Be-Lo to protest the supermarket's wage and hiring practices. Long before, Mama and Walter Green, a Coronado resident who shopped at the store, had approached the manager with a request that he hire more blacks and to allow them to cashier—and at the same wage paid to white cashiers. Evidently, the exchange did not go well. They passed out leaflets informing shoppers that 90 percent of the store's customers were Negroes, yet only 15 percent of the employees were. They also insisted that Be-Lo employ blacks at higher-paying jobs. Mr. Jordan protested in his wheelchair, and was joined by his fellow attorneys Len Holt and Ed Dawley. Len Holt traveled the South working for the Congress of Racial Equality, or CORE. He had started a chapter in Norfolk and the picketing was one of CORE's actions. More groceries are sold at Christmastime, so the protesters hoped their timing would have an impact. They even picketed on Christmas Eve. A white couple joined them on the picket line—navy Lieutenant Jay Schwartz and his wife. The lieutenant worked as a judge advocate general, so his participation was unusual.

In addition to picketing, the group asked people not to shop in the store. They had a few vehicles at their disposal, and offered to drive people elsewhere to shop. The protest continued for a month, usually on Thursday, Friday and Saturday evenings. The store ran ads in the newspaper that it was giving away cotton candy and hot dogs to children, as a way to encourage parents to shop at the store. Finally, the owner sought a temporary injunction to stop the protests, which a magistrate granted.

The seven people restrained from protesting were attorneys Joseph Jordan, Ed Dawley, and Len Holt, and citizens Evelyn Butts, Linwood Branch, Carolyn Branch and Mrs. Jay Schwartz. The store owner mischaracterized the issue as a request "not to employ persons because of their capacity or ability, regardless of race or color, but to employ persons of the Negro race solely because they are Negroes." He complained about the protesters engaging in shouts and loud persuasions so that the atmosphere outside the store made customers loath to enter.

Jordan, Dawley and Holt filed a petition to modify the injunction, because prohibiting someone from distributing handbills or publishing notices in the newspaper violated the First Amendment. A judge commented at a hearing that, by state law, the only justified picketing would involve employees who worked at the store. The petition was denied, and a court date was set.

In March, the injunction was made permanent after a hearing where numerous people testified. The store owner presented witnesses opposed to the protest. The defense presented neighbors in favor of it. The attorney for the store owner called my mother "Butts" until Mr. Dawley told him to call her Mrs. Butts and stop insulting her. The attorney then called her Evelyn Butts, refusing to address her as Mrs. Butts, though he referred to the white female witness as Mrs. Schwartz. The protest had affected the store's bottom line, with the owner claiming that his profits dropped by 90 percent.

Lieutenant Schwartz testified that he had the "unpleasant experience" of watching someone try to run down his pregnant wife with an automobile. The strangest testimony came from a minister, Reverend Gray of Mount Gilead Baptist Church, who reported that his church of seven hundred members did not approve of the protest. He said that Mr. Dawley swore at him and he "considered getting a hammer and coming after him but yielded to milder impulses" after Dawley apologized.

So it was that my mother and her friends were barred from picketing the store any longer. But, as it happened, Miss Josephine was promoted to full-time cashier at the same wage as the white cashiers. Eventually, Be-Lo hired more blacks.

Then, as now, picketing and protesting were not universally popular. The NAACP's Norfolk branch was not the type of organization to stage a protest. Its members weren't inclined to take to the streets, and the president did not approve of picketing Be-Lo. That is the reason that Len Holt started a chapter of CORE: He believed Norfolk needed other civil rights groups that believed in the power of protest. The younger activists, believing that change needed to happen quickly, and willing to put their bodies at risk to achieve their goals, did not want to be stifled by the NAACP's conservatism and caution.

A Norfolk protest that gained some national attention was held at Foreman Field, at the local campus of the College of William and Mary. Every year before football season started, the Kiwanis Club sponsored an exhibition game between the Washington Redskins and the Baltimore Colts. In 1961, Mama and quite a few of her friends protested the game, citing three problems. First, the seating in the stands was segregated. Second, the Washington Redskins, alone among NFL teams, refused to hire black players. And lastly, the Kiwanis Club was an all-white organization, and here was hosted by a state-supported facility. The Colts made it known they were not going to participate if the seating remained segregated. The NAACP met with the Colts' management and, assured the stands would include no "colored" section, announced it would not support a demonstration at the event. Messrs. Jordan, Dawley, and Holt believed making a fuss was necessary, however—and moreover, they put the name and phone number of the NAACP president, Robert D. Robertson, on their flyer announcing the protest, and directed people to call him. Robertson got an injunction to prevent its distribution.

Mama brought my sisters and me to the protest, and at twelve years old I carried a sign for the first time. There is a photograph of me with my mother's friend Rowena Warren Stancil. She held a sign that said, "$50,000 Reward For The First Black Kiwanis In Norfolk." My sign said, "In War We Fight Together. Why Not Sit Together In Peace?" Before the game, two black players on the Colts team, Lenny Moore and Johnny Sample, came out to talk to us while we were protesting. Then they went back inside and helped the Colts trample the Redskins, 41-7.

The rift between the activists in the street and the NAACP's local leadership came to a head in 1960, when Mr. Jordan was a member of the group's executive board and my mother was the board's secretary. Elections were held for officers in December 1960, but the membership didn't get word of the vote and Robert D. Robertson was reelected president. He had held the office since 1949. My mother, Mr. Jordan and a few dozen other members were livid that this election was held in virtual secrecy. They notified the national headquarters that the NAACP's own rules for holding an election had been violated. The national office invalidated the election results and ordered Norfolk to hold a new election the following March.

My mother ran for president, and the vice-presidential candidate was Julius Roberts. The candidates for secretary and treasurer were John A. Golden, Jr. and Alice Green, respectively. The executive board slate was George Banks, Mr. Jordan's sister Minnie Brownson, Norman Cofer, Mabel Cradle, J.D. Gill, Alveta and Walter Green, Lillian Green, Melvin Green, Leonard Harris, Rachel Harris, Joseph Hassell, Sr., Robert Jones, Mr. Jordan's mother Agnes Jordan, Lucille Olds, and Louberta Woody.

Robert D. Robertson immediately criticized the slate as a "militant group of dissident members." An article in the *Journal and Guide* highlighted the recent accomplishments of the NAACP under his leadership, including desegregation of schools, buses, lunch counters and tea rooms. The chapter received an award at the national convention for being the most outstanding branch. Even though the national headquarters had ordered a new election, the national and state executive secretaries, Roy Wilkins and Lester Banks, made it known that they wanted Robertson reelected. The *Journal and Guide* article quoted Robertson saying that peaceful negotiation was his preferred method of action, and that the NAACP would not become "out-and-out radicals because three or four members of this branch wish us to be so."

My mother sent a letter to the members explaining why the so-called "militant" slate was the right choice:

It is impossible for a Negro in the South to be radical. The mere fact that he is alive is conclusive proof that he is conservative.

Regardless of how this election comes out, I think a service has been rendered our organization and the citizens of Norfolk by our slate of candidates, in giving the people this democratic opportunity to end dictatorial practices. What will you do with this opportunity? What are the issues? It has been said that those of us who desire free elections are radical.

Is it radical to ask that the members be informed when elections are held; to ask that fair, honest and democratic elections be conducted in which any member may run for office if he chooses to do so; to ask that the financial records be shown to members and all funds accounted for? Is it radical to ask that the presiding officer treat with courtesy and respect all members who desire to take the floor at meetings and express their opinions, especially the elderly ladies and gentlemen?

Is it radical to inquire into how NAACP officers can take the membership fees of the members and claim to fight our enemies one day, support that same enemy the next day, again collect our membership fees another day, and support that enemy the next day—and so on? Is it radical to place a higher premium on justice, honesty, fairness, morality, and Christianity than on peace?

Is it radical to cause the racial signs to be removed from the new Public Safety Building so that our Negro citizens will not be embarrassed when they go there to transact business?

Is it radical to insist that credit be properly given to our young courageous students and children, who suffer jailing, violence and intimidation to bring about changes for our benefit? Is it radical to insist that this credit not be stolen from the young students and taken by uncourageous persons, claiming to have accomplished these benefits by "peaceful negotiations"?

Is it radical to use our efforts to secure employment for Negroes free from discriminatory bars, and not be either ashamed or afraid to engage in peaceful picketing so that Negroes can work and buy food for their children like any other citizen? Is Mr. Roy W. Wilkins, the National Executive Secretary, and the National Board of Directors, who removed the officers of the local branch, radical—are they radical for wanting the Norfolk Chapter to be one they can be proud of?

Is it radical to dream of and work for a City where Negroes are citizens, free and proud, living peacefully and in prosperity, in good times and bad times, and participating in every area of life? Are these things radical?

We admit that we are militant in fighting for the civil rights of Negro citizens. The NAACP is supposed to be a militant organization. It was founded for this purpose.

Because many of us, on account of our jobs, our families, or other reasons, cannot be militant, the NAACP was established to be militant for us. If the NAACP is not going to be militant, why do we need it? We already have peaceful social clubs, card clubs and fraternal organizations.

The most important issue in this election, my fellow members, is that stated by the words of Our Lord, "Ye cannot serve two masters." Weigh these words when you consider the inaction and the conduct of the present administration.

It is time for a change to an administration that can lead the NAACP in bringing to the Negroes of Norfolk "Peace with Justice and Honor" so that there can be a New Frontier in Race Relations.

We invite you to attend the election on Monday, March 13 at 8 p.m., Second Calvary Baptist Church, Corprew and Godfrey avenues. We ask you to support the Militant Candidates who, when elected, will remain your servants and militant warriors in the cause for freedom."

The national and state NAACP leaders continued their advocacy of Robertson. His attorney solicited telegrams of support from the leadership. Additional articles of support for Robertson appeared in the paper. In protest of this "unprecedented meddling in local affairs," the entire militant slate withdrew from the contest. "This very conflict arises out of our struggle to end the dictatorial and cynical manner in which our branch is operating," my mother told a reporter. "We cannot accept a situation in which we must tolerate a dictatorship which is allegedly fighting for democracy and justice, regardless of what national or state official intervenes." She encouraged the membership to refrain from participating in a "fixed" election.

The dissidents did not leave the NAACP. They stayed around to be a thorn in its side. One of my mother's favorite troublemakers was Ed Dawley, who had a flair for protest even when he was the only one participating. In 1957, he filed suit to desegregate toilets in the city's courthouse. Norfolk officials responded by claiming that the signs were "invitations" for colored persons to use one room and white persons another. Unbelievably, the same Judge Hoffman who had presided over the school desegregation case could not find a basis in the law for removing "white" and "colored" signs from a government building dedicated to the administration of justice.

One of Dawley's protests that bordered on performance art occurred in 1958, when he, his wife Eleanor, her mother, his brother-in-law Walter Green, and others marched in downtown Norfolk Church Street wearing green togas. Dawley gave a speech at the Community Political Club explaining that the marchers were Renaissance Disciples calling the black community to a rebirth. "The Negro community does not suffer from a lack of genius, brilliance, intelligence, plans and programs," he said. "The Disciples believe what is needed is the creation and existence of the proper community climate, atmosphere and attitude in which the genius of the Negro community can flourish in unity, in which some of the good plans and programs can receive unified support and have some chance of success."

The best Ed Dawley story occurred that summer at the state Republican Convention at Richmond's traditionally whites-only John Marshall Hotel. Dawley arrived by bus late after midnight. He called the hotel from the bus station and was told there was a vacancy. However, when he arrived at the hotel, no room was available. Dawley and the hotel management told contradictory stories about what happened next. Dawley claimed that he stripped down to his underwear in the lobby and lay down to sleep on a sofa, and was awakened about two hours later and given a key to a very nice room. Not only that, he said, the hotel did not charge him when he checked out after the convention. The management said that Dawley arrived around 4 a.m., and that the hotel had no vacancies. He was given a room early in the morning when another guest checked out. The hotel manager insisted Dawley did not take off his clothes in the lobby.

Ed Dawley left Norfolk and eventually wound up in California, where he continued his protest and his law practice more comfortably than in Virginia. My mother missed him, but continued to work in his spirit. She was always circulating a petition against some injustice. I only have two samples in my files. One is a petition to the postmaster to reassign Oakwood's postman due to his "hostile and disrespectful attitude." He was reassigned. The other is a petition to install additional street lighting in our neighborhood.

Mama's friend Alveta Green described her petition prowess in an interview in 2007. "She had an army of folks that she could just send petitions to. When anything came up, she had somebody, some man with a car, one of her drivers, and she could say, 'Go take this petition to this one and that one,' and she knew we would get it done. We were like her army."

Little did she know her greatest battle was just around the corner: abolishing state poll taxes that had long prevented blacks and poor people from participating in democracy in America.

CHAPTER SIX

SETTING THE STAGE

Numbers and statistics tell the story of black political participation in Virginia. Twenty-five blacks were elected to attend the state's constitutional convention after the Civil War. Eighty-seven were elected as representatives to the General Assembly between 1867 and 1895. One black candidate was elected to Congress from Virginia in 1889. After that, not a single black was elected to serve in the state legislature until 1968. No blacks attended the constitutional convention of 1901-1902. Virginia elected its second black Congressman in 1993—more than one hundred years after the first. The erasure of black electoral participation in Virginia was not an accident, and it would not be re-established without a fight. My mother and Mr. Jordan were two of the leading figures who waged the battle.

Mr. Jordan had often spoken of a "third force" in Virginia politics—the mass of voters disfranchised by the poll tax. In 1958 he launched an organization by that name, dedicated to eliminating the poll tax and, in the meantime, helping others register in spite of it. My mother and her friends were the backbone of this organization and called themselves the Women of Virginia's Third Force. My mother was president and Alice Green, vice president. Mr. Jordan also brought together the Norfolk Alliance of Political Action Committees, comprising fifty-two organizations and headquartered at his office.

Also in 1958, as part of Massive Resistance, the General Assembly approved a bill requiring Virginians to fill out a blank sheet of paper to register to vote. In the presence of a registrar, each was expected to write, in his or her own handwriting, the following items: name, age, date of birth, place of birth, address, current occupation, occupation for one year prior, whether he or she had voted before, and if so, the state, county, and precinct where that vote had occurred. Registrants had to know this information by rote. The registrar was not allowed to answer any questions to help the resident fill out the blank sheet of paper.

In response to the new law, The Women of Virginia's Third Force held classes in Mr. Jordan's office on how to fill out the blank sheet. Around fifty women worked with the Third Force. They did not consider themselves radicals, though other people might have seen them that way. They were mothers, wives, and church-going ladies—including Joe Jordan's mother, Agnes, and his sisters Minnie Brownson, Anna Lee Brinkley, and Agnes Gould. My mother was no ceremonial president. She was the driving force behind much of the activity the group undertook, such as registering voters, making sure people paid the poll tax, making sure they knew about the candidates running for office, and most of all, getting voters to the polls on election day.

In February 1959, a flyer from Virginia's Third Force was distributed in the fourth and fifth precincts. "If you," it said, "are what we think you are—one of those 20th CENTURY, ATOMIC AGE NEGROES, who believes in STANDING UP and FIGHTING FOR HIS RIGHTS—Then you are the person we are looking for. We're tired of discrimination—We're tired of segregation—We're tired of poor streets and bad lighting—We're tired of INSULTS from Mayor Duckworth and Governor Almond. We're tired of the whole political MESS in Virginia, and we want to—and CAN do something about it. WITH YOUR HELP." The flyer promised that the Third Force would qualify every Negro "so WE ALL can VOTE."

The NAACP bought a 1948 Oldsmobile, dubbed the Vote Mobile, that was used to register voters throughout Norfolk. It was painted with slogans such as, "Pay Poll Tax," "Let's All Vote," and "Virginia's Third Force." The Oldsmobile was equipped with a public-address system. When it rolled through black neighborhoods, its occupants encouraging residents to vote, it was not a subtle presence.

In 1959, Mr. Jordan ran for General Assembly from Norfolk as a write-in candidate. That spring, he had organized a voters' rally at the Municipal Auditorium attended by some 1,500 people. Adam Clayton Powell was one of the featured speakers. The Women of Virginia's Third Force helped him organize and sponsor the event. The Vote Mobile drove all over Norfolk to spread awareness of the rally. I remember vividly when Mr. Jordan came down our street. Though he was normally soft spoken and erudite, his voice boomed all over our neighborhood telling everyone to write his name on the ballot.

Norfolk's registrar refused to allow Mr. Jordan to look at the voter registration books. He asked all three members of the Electoral Board for permission to inspect the rolls and they, too, refused him. He was told that he could submit twenty names he wanted checked, and the registrar would comply at her convenience. Mr. Holt and Mr. Dawley filed a lawsuit on his behalf, claiming that voter registration rolls are public records similar to property deeds, which anyone could examine. The judge agreed. My mother went downtown to the election office and copied thousands of names by hand for a couple of months. "But, down in the registrar's office, they had segregation down there," Mama said. The white and black voters' cards were kept in separate files. White people's names were on white cards and black people's names were on yellow cards. From the list my mother transcribed, the Third Force built a database of voters that helped the group devise a strategy to reach out to unregistered voters.

On election day, Mr. Jordan received almost a thousand votes, but many were disqualified: Voters had failed, the officials said, to properly mark their ballots. A year later, Mr. Jordan's name was on the ballot for City Council. He lost that race, too. These experiences reinforced his belief that more blacks needed to vote if blacks were to be elected.

The poll tax stood as the major impediment preventing that from happening. As recently as 1951, a Virginia case challenging the poll tax had gone all the way to the U.S. Supreme Court. *Butler v. Thompson* had been dismissed, the justices citing a 1937 case, *Breedlove v. Suttles*, as precedent. Both cases had held that poll taxes were not discriminatory, as the U.S. Constitution clearly gave states the right to set eligibility requirements for voting.

In addition to running for office, Mr. Jordan formed a law partnership with Edward Dawley and Leonard Holt in 1960.

The aggressive civil rights work undertaken by Jordan, Dawley and Holt would last for only two years, but in that time the firm litigated cases in every state of the former Confederacy. Their work included three death penalty suits, thirty felony cases and an astounding two thousand misdemeanors. They also pursued six integration lawsuits.

The quick demise of the partnership can be directly blamed on the Virginia Committee on Offenses Against the Administration of Justice. Jordan, Dawley and Holt was served with a writ in September 1961 requiring the firm to turn over all papers "used as a means for violating the common and statutory laws of Virginia." The committee considered the lawyers' work with the Congress of Racial Equality (CORE), the Southern Christian Leadership Conference (SCLC), the Student Non-Violent Coordinating Committee (SNCC), and any other clients working for civil rights, to be grounds for investigation.

Jordan, Dawley and Holt refused to be intimidated. The firm sent a letter to the committee chairman, J.C. Hutcheson, stating "Neither you nor your agents will ever be allowed to look at any records belonging to our clients. In the best American tradition of freedom, we defy you." The committee was likewise not intimidated, and continued to press the issue until the firm was spurred to bring a class action lawsuit against it. The expense of fighting the suit forced the firm to dissolve in 1962. Dawley and Holt left Virginia, and the matter was not resolved until 1965.

In the same year that the committee raided Jordan, Dawley and Holt's law office to stop its civil rights work, a commission was appointed by the General Assembly to study Virginia's election laws. It found that the "blank sheet" was causing a breakdown in the registration of new voters. As much as an hour was required to register them. The blank sheet angered white voters, especially the elderly. The commission was told that "colored citizens have held classes and come in prepared to fill out the registration forms, but white people are getting confused." In 1962, the General Assembly put a constitutional amendment on the ballot to eliminate the blank sheet. The voters passed the resolution. One noxious impediment to voter registration was gone, yet the most damaging remained.

Mr. Jordan, now a solo practitioner, decided to sue to abolish state poll taxes in Virginia. He had picked a plaintiff, an elderly friend of his father named Timberlake, who earned his living by making deliveries with a horse and wagon. When Mr. Timberlake became ill, my mother stepped into history.

The raid on his firm's office and the subsequent investigation affected Mr. Jordan's relationship with my mother. He realized he was viewed as a threat by the political establishment. He worried that his phone might be tapped. Whenever they had anything important to discuss, anything of a strategic nature, he would drive to our house and Mama would go out to his car to talk in private. After his death, his family obtained his FBI file, and the contents confirmed that Mr. Jordan was under surveillance.

Mr. Jordan and Len Holt worked on their poll tax brief in 1963. In August, my mother went to the March on Washington to hear Martin Luther King speak. Norfolk's NAACP had chartered three buses. While she wouldn't have missed it for the world, she didn't enjoy the bus ride or the heat. From the grass in front of the Lincoln Memorial, she could not see the Supreme Court building, but she hoped to see it one day soon. In the late fall, Mr. Jordan's brief challenging Virginia's poll tax was nearly ready for filing. In November, an article appeared in the *Journal and Guide* announcing a new Norfolk chapter of the Southern Christian Leadership Conference. Mr. Jordan was treasurer and my mother, secretary. Martin Luther King sent the chapter a letter of congratulations, welcoming its members into the fight for voting rights. Then, on November 22, President John F. Kennedy was assassinated in Dallas, Texas.

I was in ninth-grade science class at Rosemont Junior High when the teacher shared the news that the president had been shot. It was the last class of the day, and a Friday. We couldn't concentrate on science. At 2:38 p.m., Walter Cronkite, the TV news anchor on CBS, reported that President Kennedy was dead. The airwaves were filled with news of the assassination. The school released us early.

The very next day, a Saturday, my mother went to Mr. Jordan's office to sign the legal brief for the poll tax lawsuit. It was notarized by his sister, M.J. Brownson. Shock over the assassination was palpable. What would have seemed momentous on a personal level—being a plaintiff in a lawsuit to advance voting rights—now paled in comparison to the events in Dallas. Yet, my mother and Mr. Jordan knew they had to press forward. On Sunday, while many Americans were in church, Lee Harvey Oswald, the accused assassin, was shot and killed by Jack Ruby in the basement of the Dallas Police Department's headquarters. My mother was not a churchgoer—she always stayed home on Sunday mornings to make fried chicken and rolls and the best brown gravy in the world, and her closest friends would stop by after services. That particular Sunday, their conversation centered on the assassination. The America they thought they knew had changed overnight.

Local news stations reported that school would be cancelled on Monday for the president's funeral. I watched it on television with my parents and my grandfather. They all cried. My mother and father could not understand why anyone would kill President Kennedy. He was forward thinking and seemed a friend to blacks, and the news struck the African-American community especially hard. The new president, Lyndon B. Johnson, was a Texan with a reputation for old-fashioned Southern attitudes. What kind of a friend would he be?

Two days after Kennedy's funeral, President Johnson made his first address to a joint session of Congress. He told the legislators, "No memorial oration or eulogy could more eloquently honor President Kennedy's memory than the earliest possible passage of the civil rights bill for which he fought so long." The next day, a raw, anxious nation observed the Thanksgiving holiday. On Friday, November 29, Mr. Jordan went to the federal courthouse in Norfolk to file *Mrs. Evelyn Butts v. Governor Albertis Harrison, et. al.*

The adoption of poll taxes was inextricably linked to white backlash against Reconstruction, an era that lasted from the end of the Civil War, in 1865, to 1877, when the federal government ended its postwar occupation of the South. Immediately following the war, emboldened by President Andrew Johnson's lenient attitude toward former Confederates, Southern states passed "black codes" restricting freed blacks' rights. In 1866, the Republican-dominated Congress responded by passing a civil rights bill guaranteeing equal rights to all persons born in the United States. Johnson vetoed the bill, causing Congress to override a presidential veto for the first time in U.S. history.

That same year, Congress passed the Fourteenth Amendment, which similarly holds that, "All persons born or naturalized in the United States, and subject to the jurisdiction thereof, are citizens of the United States and of the State wherein they reside." No state, the amendment declares, "shall make or enforce any law which shall abridge the privileges or immunities of citizens of the United States; nor shall any State deprive any person of life, liberty, or property, without due process of law; nor deny to any person within its jurisdiction the equal protection of the laws." Southern states were required to ratify the Amendment to be readmitted to the Union.

In 1867, Congress passed a Reconstruction bill, again over Johnson's veto, temporarily establishing five military districts in the South with instructions as to how the governments they oversaw should be run. In 1868, the Fourteenth Amendment was ratified by the states. In 1869, Congress passed the Fifteenth Amendment, guaranteeing that no citizen would be denied the right to vote "on account of race, color, or previous condition of servitude." For the first time, Southern blacks were elected to public office, and even to Congress.

By 1870, all the former Confederate states had been readmitted to the Union and the Fifteenth Amendment was ratified. Other legislation passed during Reconstruction included state-funded public school systems and laws banning racial discrimination in public transport and public places. New laws aimed to create more equitable taxation, improve railroads, and fund economic development to rebuild a region torn apart by war. During those revolutionary five years between 1865 and 1870, white supremacists rejected the Republican experiment to create an egalitarian society. Organizations such as the Ku Klux

Klan, White League, and the Knights of White Camelia used violence against Republican leaders, black and white. Night raids, beatings, and arson were all used to intimidate blacks and their white supporters. Even though Ulysses S. Grant's administration passed a law in 1871—colloquially called the Ku Klux Klan Act—authorizing the president to declare martial law and use military force to suppress terrorist organizations, the will to support Reconstruction waned. This fatigue was exacerbated by an economic depression in 1874 that caused widespread poverty in the South. That year, the Democratic Party won back the House of Representatives for the first time since the war's end.

In spite of the Ku Klux Klan Act, gangs of whites in Vicksburg, Mississippi, killed three hundred blacks in a riot to suppress black voting in 1874. The town's black sheriff fled to the state capital. President Grant sent a company of troops to insure the sheriff's return. He was subsequently murdered by his white deputy. A paramilitary organization called the Red Shirts operated openly as the "military arm of the Democratic Party." During the summer, the governor requested that Grant send troops to quell the continuing violence. The president declined—a declaration of martial law undoubtedly would have been an issue in the upcoming election. In 1874, Republicans cast 30,000 more votes than Democrats in Mississippi. In 1875, Democrats cast 30,000 more votes than Republicans. Violence was working to control the vote.

In 1876, Republican presidential candidate Rutherford B. Hayes agreed to a compromise with Congressional Democrats. They agreed to certify him as president in a contested election, and he agreed to Democratic control of the South. U.S. Army troops were withdrawn from the former Confederate states in

1877. Reconstruction was officially over.

In Virginia, the state constitution was amended in 1876 to deny the right to vote based on non-payment of a poll tax. A second amendment disfranchised men who had criminal convictions. These two amendments significantly reduced the number of black men who were eligible to vote. Between 1889 and 1910, eleven states in the South adopted the poll tax.

Finally, in 1896, the U.S. Supreme Court codified the segregation of black citizens. The Court ruled in *Plessy v. Ferguson* that the existence of "separate but equal" spheres for blacks and whites was constitutional. The era of Jim Crow obtained an official blessing.

Virginia convened a constitutional convention for a full year, from June 1901 to June 1902. One hundred delegates, dominated by Democrats but including eleven Republicans and one Independent, debated over its course. The convention president, John Goode, opened the proceedings by admitting without embarrassment that a fundamental purpose of the gathering was to prevent Negroes from voting without violating the Fifteenth Amendment to the U.S. Constitution.

Mr. Jordan attached long sections of the convention speeches in his brief for my mother, illustrating to the federal court that poll taxes were intended to disenfranchise blacks. Here is Goode in his own words, describing the convention:

> *Now, I repeat, our people have no prejudice, no animosity against the members of the colored race... the dominant party in Congress not only committed a stupendous blunder, but a crime against civilization and Christianity, when against the advice of their wisest leaders, they re-*

quired the people of Virginia and the South, under the rule of bayonet, to submit to universal negro suffrage.

The negro had just emerged from a state of slavery, he had no education, he had no experience in the duties of citizenship. He had no qualification for participation in the functions of government. The all-powerful Creator, for some wise purpose, had made him inferior to the white man, and ever since the dawn of history, as the pictured monuments of Egypt attest, he had occupied a position of inferiority. In the language of an eminent Virginian... he had founded no empire, he had built no towered city, invented no art, discovered no truth, bequeathed no everlasting possession to the future through law giver, hero, bard, benefactor of mankind.

What, then, was the origin of the movement for constitutional revision in Virginia? It had its origin in the consciousness of the people of Virginia that negro enfranchisement was a crime to begin with and a wretched failure to the end, and that the unlawful but necessary expedients to preserve us from the evil effects of the thing were debauching the morals and intellect of our own race.

The primary purpose of that convention was to abridge the right of popular suffrage and to eliminate every negro of whom we could be rid without running counter to the prohibition of the Federal Constitution. Not a white man in Virginia, nor a black man of ordinary intelligence, will contend that this purpose of constitutional revision was disguised or attempted to be concealed.

To a layperson untrained in the law, this blatant public admission would be adequate moral justification for abolishing Virginia's poll tax. Disfranchising blacks seems to have been the whole point of the tax! But a court cannot consider the intent of the legislators. It is a settled legal principle that the text of the law itself is all a judge can interpret.

The poll tax law of Virginia stated, in part, "Every citizen of the United States, having the qualifications of age and residence required in section eighteen, shall be entitled to register provided that he has personally paid to the proper officer all State poll taxes legally assessed or assessable against him for the three years next proceeding that in which he offers to register." The statute did not include the word "negro," so the stated intent of the constitutional convention and the speeches of the delegates were irrelevant. Overturning the poll tax in court would require finding an avenue of attack on the written words alone.

The legal precedent establishing state poll taxes as constitutional was *Breedlove v. Suttles*, a 1937 case. Nolen Breedlove was a white, twenty-eight-year-old Georgia man who attempted to register to vote in 1936. He refused to pay his accrued poll taxes (and probable penalties), a sum which amounted to $13.50. The tax collector, Suttles, refused to register him, stating that the tax of one dollar per year was an obligation for all inhabitants between twenty-one and sixty years of age. The only persons exempt from the tax were women, who did not register to vote, and the blind.

Breedlove did not claim he was too poor to pay the tax, but the amount was substantial in 1936 dollars. "At that time, $13.50 could have fed a family for a long time," legal scholar Ronnie L. Podolefsky observed in 1998 in the Columbia *Journal* of Gender and Law. That amount "might have filled a pantry with all of the following: fifty pounds of grits, twenty-five loaves of bread, ten dozen eggs, twenty pounds of pork and beans, ten pounds of lamb shoulder, five pounds of chuck roast, and fifty pounds each of potatoes, yams, and cabbage. Even during later periods, the tax might amount to a day's wages for some. If the tax went unpaid for a few years, some individuals would need to give the tax collector a sum representing several week's wages."

Breedlove found an attorney, J. Ira Harrelson, who was willing to litigate on his behalf. They argued that poll taxes violated the equal protection clause and the privileges and immunities clause of the Fourteenth Amendment. Privileges and immunities allow citizens to travel freely among the states, to become full citizens of any state, and to be free of discrimination when they visit another state. The concept was intended to build a sense of national citizenship.

In a novel twist, they argued further that the poll tax violated the Nineteenth Amendment because it states that the right to vote shall not be denied "on account of sex." Men between twenty-one and sixty were singled out to pay the tax.

The court swept away all the arguments in a terse 1,188-word opinion. The equal protection clause did not apply because the clause "does not require absolute equality." People over sixty years of age are often exempted from jury duty, road work or service in a militia. The poll tax exemption for the elderly was no different than these other exemptions. Women could be exempted because of "the burdens necessarily borne by them for the preservation of the race." Furthermore, the laws of Georgia declared the husband to be the head of the family and the wife to be subject to him. No need to add to the husband's burden by requiring him to pay the tax for her.

The privileges and immunities clause did not apply because the privilege of voting was not derived from the United States, but was conferred by the state. Therefore, the court ruled, a state might "condition suffrage as it deems appropriate," except where forbidden by the Fifteenth and Nineteenth amendments.

The court reasoned that the Nineteenth Amendment had nothing to do with taxes—it simply forbade denying a citizen the right to vote based on sex. Poll taxes had been in existence in Georgia for more than a century, dating to the colonial period. Requiring payment of the tax prior to registration did not specifically deny men between the age of twenty-one and sixty the right to vote. "Power to levy and power to collect are equally necessary," the court wrote.

The year *Breedlove* was decided, 1937, was a year like no other for the U.S. Supreme Court. Franklin Delano Roosevelt had been elected to his second term as president. He needed electoral support for his New Deal programs which would largely benefit poor whites. He wrote in a memo, "One difficulty is that three quarters of the whites in the South cannot vote—poll tax, etc." To Roosevelt, the poll tax was not a racial issue. It was economic.

Roosevelt had coined the word "Polltaxia" to describe the South and was making poll-tax abolition a key progressive demand. New Deal supporters in Florida, Georgia's neighbor, were pushing to repeal the tax there.

In February1937, legislation was introduced to increase the number of Supreme Court Justices to as many as fifteen, as well as increasing in the number of judges in other federal courts. Some saw the bill as Roosevelt's attempt to "pack" the Supreme Court with Justices who would approve New Deal legislation. The bill was unpopular, but it might have had some effect on the existing court. In March, its justices handed down a decision approving a minimum wage law in Washington state, just two years after striking down a similar law in New York. The next month, it upheld the National Labor Relations Act. In May, it found the Social Security Act constitutional. All were huge victories for Roosevelt. The Supreme Court had a reputation for hostility to interventionist government. Its decisions in early 1937 marked a shift in its thinking.

The court reform bill was not to be one of Roosevelt's victories. The Senate Judiciary Committee disapproved it. The bill was rewritten to eliminate the provision increasing the size of the Supreme Court. The justices left for the summer recess, able to put the prospect of an expanded court behind them. During the subsequent term, in December 1937, *Breedlove* was decided, upholding Georgia's right to "condition suffrage as it deems appropriate." The court sent the message that if poll taxes were to be abolished in Georgia—or any state—they should be abolished by the state.

Two notable personalities were present for the events of 1937 who would also play a part in the poll tax question in the 1960s. *Breedlove* was one of the first cases decided by Justice Hugo Black, a native of Alabama, and he would still be on the Court in 1966 when the issue of poll taxes returned. A Florida state senator, Spessard Holland, supported abolishing Florida's poll tax during the Depression because the move would enfranchise poor whites likely to vote for him. Florida did abolish its poll tax in 1938 and Holland became a U.S. senator in 1946. He would become a major figure in poll tax legislation over three decades.

After the Breedlove setback, the NAACP joined forces with other voting rights organizations to form the Southern Conference for Human Welfare (SCHW) in 1938. The coalition quickly came up with a two-pronged legal and political strategy against the poll tax. In 1939, it chose a white man from Tennessee as a plaintiff to challenge the poll tax, but the Court refused to grant certiorari. Its political strategy aimed to abolish the poll tax through legislation. California Representative Lee Geyer sponsored a bill focusing on corrupt politicians who bought and sold poll tax receipts, sullying the integrity of the election process. In 1942, his initiative passed in the House but was defeated in a filibuster led by Southern conservatives in the Senate. The House would pass poll tax abolition bills five times during the 1940s. All failed in the upper chamber.

In Virginia, Governor James Price proposed in 1938 and 1940 that the poll tax be reduced from $1.50 to $1, but the initiative was defeated by the General Assembly. A report written for the Virginia Advisory Legislative Council by distinguished University of Virginia political scientist Robert Gooch highlighted the political corruption inherent in block payments of the tax and the refusal of some registrars to register African Americans. The Advisory Council did not so much as dignify his report by printing it. After World War II, Governor Colgate W. Darden Jr. and his fellow progressives proposed repealing the poll tax as an embarrassing impediment to democracy. In 1949, however, an amendment to Virginia's constitution that hewed to such thinking was proposed and defeated in a referendum.

The next step taken by anti-poll tax activists was to create a single-issue lobbying organization, the National Committee to Abolish the Poll Tax, which took pains not to conflate its efforts with the related struggle for black voting rights. Active from 1942 to 1948, the group stayed true to its New Deal roots, emphasizing class, not race, as a strategy. It estimated that the poll tax eliminated three whites for every two black voters.

There were small successes. The wartime Congress passed the Soldier Vote Act of 1942, which relieved soldiers voting by absentee ballot from paying a poll tax. Even Southern conservatives could not oppose such a bill. The Supreme Court struck down the notion of "white primary" elections in 1944. Georgia abolished its state poll tax in 1945. In 1951, Tennessee abolished its state poll tax and a Virginia case, Butler v. Thompson, made its way to the Supreme Court.

Jesse Butler, a black woman, sued local officials in Arlington in civil court for failing to register her to vote. She cited as grounds Virginia's 1902 constitutional convention and its stated purpose of disenfranchising Negroes through a poll tax. She also claimed that even if the poll tax statutes were fair on their face and seemingly non-discriminatory against Negroes, they were administered by local officials in such a way that they did discriminate. Her attorney presented statistics to show that 15 percent fewer Negroes than whites were assessed for the tax. The U.S. District Court for the Eastern District of Virginia found no fault with the way local officials performed their duties, and complimented the defendant Thompson for her appearance, her manner of testifying, and her frankness, adding that her candor made an "unusually favorable impression." The District Court defended the 1902 convention, stating that even the most violent delegates "expressed an intention to bring about this result by means that were valid under the Federal Constitution." The Court claimed there wasn't a "shred of evidence" in the record that a Negro had been refused assessment or that any white person had been permitted to vote without paying this poll taxes. The fact that fewer Negroes were assessed was attributable to the fact that their names might not appear in telephone directories, on the property tax rolls, or in the motor vehicle registration records. Butler's attorney was so outraged, he told the *The New York Times* he had "asked withdrawal of his name as a member of the bar of the United States Supreme Court." At this point, the courts did not seem to be the avenue through which state poll taxes would be abolished.

Two years later, the appointment of Earl Warren as Chief Justice of the Supreme Court marked a watershed moment in American law and society. Within one year, the Warren Court decided *Brown v. Board of Education,* forcing desegregation in public schools and providing a catapult for the Civil Rights movement.

In 1955, the Montgomery bus boycott began. In 1956, segregation in public transit was declared unconstitutional. In 1957 and 1960, Congress passed Civil Rights bills which dealt primarily with measures to ensure voting rights. Only 20 percent of African Americans were registered to vote. The 1957 bill set up a Civil Rights Commission to investigate instances where citizens had been deprived of their right to vote. It changed the rules for serving on federal juries, allowing citizens who were not registered voters to be selected. It also created the Civil Rights

Division in the Department of Justice. The 1960 bill required local jurisdictions to keep voting records that could be inspected by the government for evidence of discrimination against certain groups. Obviously, Congress recognized that something was very wrong with voting in America.

Mr. Jordan was hopeful that growing public sentiment against poll taxes, both state and federal, would bolster his case against Virginia's poll tax. The Twenty-fourth Amendment abolishing federal poll taxes was passed by Congress in August of 1962. By the time he filed my mother's lawsuit, thirty-six states had voted for ratification—two shy of the needed thirty-eight votes. A battle that had begun when Franklin Roosevelt was president finally seemed winnable.

Virginia convened a special session of the General Assembly in 1963 to set new rules for how to vote in federal elections in light of the Twenty-fourth Amendment. Eight days before Mr. Jordan filed his lawsuit, the legislature passed two acts requiring federal voters to file a certificate of residency by October 1 before the year they planned to vote. This certificate had to be filed every year. The federal voter also had the option to pay the state poll tax to be allowed to vote in both state and federal elections. Virginia was not about to let the federal government dictate its election laws.

At that time, state poll taxes had been voluntarily repealed by every state except Alabama, Arkansas, Mississippi, Texas, and Virginia. Would the federal courts uphold state poll taxes as a privilege of state's rights? Or would they overturn the 1937 precedent that declared they did not violate the Equal Protection clause of the Constitution?

In 1963, the odds did not favor either side.

CHAPTER SEVEN

THE LONG JOURNEY TO WASHINGTON

In 1962, Spessard Holland, the Florida senator who'd campaigned successfully against the poll tax in his home state, triumphed in a fight he'd waged for sixteen years: He sponsored a constitutional amendment abolishing the federal poll tax and saw it adopted in both the House and Senate. "The right of citizens of the United States," the resulting Twenty-fourth Amendment held, "to vote in any primary or other election for President or Vice President, for electors for President or Vice President, or for Senator or Representative in Congress, shall not be denied or abridged by the United States or any State by reason of failure to pay any poll tax or other tax."

Spessard was a strange emissary for an amendment that would so benefit African Americans. He was a lifelong segregationist who had signed the so-called Southern Manifesto, officially called the Declaration of Constitutional Principles. It was a document written by Congress in 1956 in opposition to racial integration of public places, signed by nineteen senators and eighty-two representatives, all from the South. Spessard voted against the Civil Rights acts of 1957, 1960 and 1964. He even voted against the Voting Rights Act of 1965. But his devotion to ending federal poll taxes dated back to 1937, to its roots as a New Deal progressive idea. Like a dog with a bone, he never let it go.

Ironically, by the time the Twenty-fourth Amendment passed, it was not a welcome occurrence to civil rights activists. The NAACP, Martin Luther King, the American Jewish Congress, Americans for Democratic Action, the Anti-Defamation League, and others saw it as setting a bad precedent. If future civil rights gains had to be made through constitutional amendments—rather than through federal court decisions or congressional legislation—then it meant that thirteen states could block progress.

The civil rights activists preferred a triangular strategy. First, a popular mandate existed because a majority of the American people clearly supported ending the Jim Crow era. Second, landmark legislation must be written by Congress in support of that mandate. Third, legal precedents, what some might call super precedents, must be handed down by the Supreme Court. Ultimately, *Harper v. Virginia State Board of Elections* became that super precedent.

The complaint Mr. Jordan filed in Norfolk in November of 1963 was nine pages long, including the cover page and Mama's affidavit asking to proceed in *forma pauperis* because she did not have money to pay court costs. A complaint is the first document filed in a lawsuit. It is not the legal brief. A complaint identifies the plaintiff and defendant, states the legal issue to be resolved, and identifies which court has jurisdiction. This complaint stated that the jurisdiction of a federal court was warranted by the first, thirteenth, fourteenth, and fifteenth amendments to the U.S. Constitution, and also by Title 28 of the U.S. Code, governing the judiciary and judicial procedure, and Title 42, governing the public health and welfare.

In eleven numbered paragraphs, some no more than a sentence, Mr. Jordan laid out his new attack against the poll tax.

1. There are uncounted and unknown Negro citizens who cannot afford to pay money for anything other than food, clothing, and shelter.

2. These people constitute the class action of the suit.

3. The Plaintiff is qualified to vote except that she cannot afford to pay the poll tax.

4. Defendants will not allow Plaintiff to vote without paying the poll tax.

5. Virginia's poll tax is intended to circumvent the Fifteenth Amendment which guaranteed Negroes the right to vote.

6. Denying the right to vote by requiring the payment of a poll tax deprives citizens of their First Amendment rights to petition the government and to freedom of speech.

7. Denying Negroes the right to vote is a violation of the Thirteenth Amendment which freed the slaves, because it burdens them with a badge of slavery—the arbitrary denial of the right to participate in government.

8. The poll tax violates the Fourteenth Amendment, equal protection of the laws, because it affords to those with money rights which are denied to the poor.

9. By law, Virginia's poll tax payment lists are segregated by race. Officials who do not keep separate lists are punished and fined, evidence that discrimination is the point of the law.

10. Widows of Confederate soldiers are exempt from the tax, recognizing that the tax is a hardship for those without means. The poll tax is not a lien and cannot be collected except when a citizen wishes to vote.

11. The constitutional convention of 1902 required ratification by the citizens. No such vote took place, therefore the laws requiring a poll tax were not laws at all.

The remaining three pages quoted the laws of Virginia and the obligations placed on officials to administer the tax. The most salient feature of the complaint was that Mr. Jordan made poverty the central argument against the poll tax. Neither *Breedlove v. Suttles*, nor Butler v. Thompson, had made that point. How would the state of Virginia counter it?

The day after Mr. Jordan filed his petition, the *Washington Post* wrote about the lawsuit. The article is interesting for what it does not explain. It acknowledged that the suit questioned the tax's legality under the Constitution and claimed the Virginia constitution was not valid because it had never been ratified by the voters. It reported that the suit called for a permanent injunction banning enforcement of poll tax laws. The newspaper noted, further, that the petition would be certified by the chief judge of the U.S. District Court, after which a three-judge panel would be appointed in the U.S. Fourth Circuit Court of Appeals to hear the case. The article pointed out that the petition made no mention of the recent legislation enacted in response to the Twenty-fourth Amendment requiring federal voters to file a certificate of residency—Mr. Jordan was quoted saying that the new legislation would be nullified by the injunction. The article quoted at length from the petition, describing my mother's poverty and the poverty of uncounted and unnamed Negroes in Virginia who were part of the class action. But the story did not explain that denying poor people the right to vote by requiring them to pay a poll tax violated the Fourteenth Amendment's equal protection clause. Was the argument so novel that the Post missed it?

A week later, the front page of Norfolk's *Journal and Guide* included a small picture of my mother and a paragraph about the lawsuit directing readers to an article on an inside page, which was essentially a reprint of the *Washington Post* story. The poll tax lawsuit shared the front page with stories both local and national witnessing the struggles of the Civil Rights movement.

FEARLESS

Above the paper's nameplate a boxed headline blared, "The ONLY Way to Get Rid of the Poll Tax is to PAY IT!" In smaller print the headline was explained. "There is only one way to get rid of the Poll Tax in Virginia! If you believe it is a burden on voters intended to make it possible for a small group of politicians to control the State, you are right. And you want it abolished. To get rid of the Poll Tax you must pay it so you can vote for those State officials and legislators who also want to get rid of it." A second headline on the bottom of the box warned, "You Must Pay Poll Taxes by Monday, Dec. 9 to Vote in June Elections." Forewarned was forearmed.

The lead article described how Virginia's Prince Edward County schools were destined to be scrutinized by the U.S. Supreme Court. The schools had been closed for more than four years to avoid court-ordered desegregation. The Virginia Supreme Court had ruled that the state constitution allowed counties, towns and cities to abandon public education if they so chose. Governor Albertis Harrison was quoted saying that Prince Edward County would reopen its schools as soon as the U.S. Supreme Court recognized that the county had a right to circumvent court-ordered desegregation.

Other stories made clear that all hell seemed to be breaking loose. Within a half-hour of President Kennedy's assassination, Roy Wilkins of the NAACP began receiving threats that he would be next. Police were guarding the NAACP's Washington offices. In Chicago, Malcolm X had been suspended from public speaking by Elijah Muhammad, leader of the Nation of Islam, over comments he'd made calling the president's assassination "chickens coming home to roost." A deeper rift between the two men in the black Muslim organization was detected. And closer to home, at least fifty students at Norfolk State University had paid the poll tax as part of a drive by the Southern Christian Leadership Conference. Martin Luther King might come to Norfolk, many hoped, to stimulate registration and voting.

Meanwhile, Protestant ministers in the National Council of Churches were told by their leadership that the future of Christianity in America would hinge on the courage that white churchmen displayed in fighting for Negro rights. "Unless churches take a convincing, effective, courageous stand on this overriding moral issue," the council held, "nothing else they do is going to count for very much."

A few days before Christmas 1963, an article about the lawsuit appeared in Norfolk's morning daily, *The Virginian-Pilot*. Virginia Attorney General Robert Button, acting on behalf of the governor, asked the three-judge panel to dismiss the poll tax suit. Another defendant, the clerk of the city's Corporation Court, asked the judges to turn the suit over to Virginia's Supreme Court of Appeals. The other two defendants, Registrar Mary Dudley and City Treasurer Alex Bell, joined the attorney general's pleas and claimed they were performing their constitutional duties in collecting the poll tax.

The attorney general moved to dismiss based on three points: He claimed that my mother lacked the capacity and standing to bring the suit. He argued that the federal court had no jurisdiction to hear the case because it attacked a state poll tax. And finally, he held that the plaintiff had not stated a legal claim upon which relief could be granted—essentially arguing that no laws had been broken, and that therefore no relief was warranted.

The *Pilot* story quoted the attorney general testily refusing to explain why Mama did not have capacity or standing: "We thought we'd let them (the plaintiff and her lawyers) worry about that for a little while. It has a very definite meaning, I'll tell you that."

The newspaper explained the constitutional grounds on which Mama's petition was based—that "the poll tax laws deny equal protection of the laws to Mrs. Butts and other Negro citizens, as guaranteed in the Fourteenth Amendment to the Constitution. Those citizens of financial means are afforded a right which is denied to the plaintiff solely because she is without financial means."

One month later, in January 1964, Maine and South Dakota became the final two states to ratify the Twenty-fourth Amendment. The news was buried on page fourteen of the *The New York Times*, along with a photo of President Johnson ceremoniously signing a certificate of ratification by three-fourths of the states. The news was greeted with little fanfare.

After Mama's lawsuit was filed, an attorney named Lawrence Speiser from the American Civil Liberties Union in Washington, D.C., contacted Mr. Jordan. He and D.C. attorney Allison Brown had four poor black plaintiffs in nearby Fairfax County, and they wanted to file a poll tax suit in federal court in Alexandria. Speiser asked for a copy of Mr. Jordan's brief and he willingly shared it. The case, filed in March 1964, was styled *Annie E. Harper et al. v. Virginia State Board of Elections, et al.*

The ACLU lawyers, all of whom were white, sued the State Board of Elections, rather than the governor, figuring that the board was directly charged with supervising and coordinating the election laws of the state. The other defendants were the

Fairfax County Board of Elections and Waneta Buckley, the general registrar of Fairfax County.

The lead plaintiff, Annie Harper, was a retired maid who in the past had worked for one of the ACLU attorneys. She was single, and her sole income was derived from Social Security. Plaintiff Gladys Berry had no regular income. She provided care for seven children—two of her own and five belonging to her two single daughters, who worked as domestics to support their mother and children. A married couple, Curtis and Myrtle Burr, were the other plaintiffs. Mr. Burr worked in construction, which is characterized by irregular employment. The couple had nine children, and Mr. Burr's income was not sufficient to pay poll taxes for himself and his wife after taking care of his family.

All of the plaintiffs in the *Butts and Harper* cases had filed affidavits requesting to proceed in *forma pauperis*—to be exempted from paying court costs because they were without financial means to pay them.

The *Butts* case was dismissed in May, but not for the three reasons cited in the defendant's motion to dismiss. Mr. Jordan had filed a long list of interrogatories for the defendant to answer regarding income and voter registration statistics for white and blacks. He filed them too late for the defendant to answer by the trial date. He filed a motion to amend his complaint six days before trial was to begin. Jordan's brief on the amended complaint was filed after the date specified in pretrial orders.

The state objected to having to answer the interrogatories. Mr. Jordan had requested statistics that would support the suit's claim that Negroes made significantly less money than whites. Voter registration figures, for instance, would show that many fewer Negroes registered to vote in Virginia. The state declined to provide the data, complaining that it would be preparing Mama's case for her. Although Mr. Jordan was willing to go to trial on the original complaint and brief, and without the interrogatories, the judge dismissed the case for failure to prosecute with due diligence. A week later, Mr. Jordan refiled the *Butts* case in U.S. District Court in Richmond.

One month later, one of the most unspeakable crimes of the civil rights era gripped the nation's attention. Three voting rights activists—David Schwerner and Andrew Goodman from New York, and James Chaney from Mississippi—disappeared while on an expedition to register black voters in Mississippi. Their burned-out station wagon was found within days of their disappearance. The nation followed the search for their bodies by hundreds of FBI agents over the next six weeks, an effort augmented by navy divers who combed swamps, rivers, and lakes—and in the process found the remains of others who had met violent ends in recent years.

Ten days into the search, as the nation prepared to celebrate the Fourth of July, President Johnson signed the Civil Rights Act of 1964 in front of television cameras. It was front-page news, but hardly greeted with happiness in the South. The *The New York Times* quoted U.S. Representative Howard W. Smith of Virginia, chairman of the House Rules Committee, saying the history of the bill was one of "heedless trampling upon the rights of citizens from the time the first bill was introduced" in June 1963. "But the bell has tolled," he said. "In a few minutes you will vote this monstrous instrument of oppression upon all of the American people.

"You have sowed the wind. Now an oppressed people are to reap the whirlwind. King, Martin Luther, not satisfied with what will then be the law of the land, has announced his purpose, with the backing of the Executive Department, to begin a series of demonstrations inevitably to be accompanied by bloodshed, violence, strife and bitterness."

That Howard Smith could ignore the fact that violence was being inflicted on people who were only seeking equal rights is typical of the era. In the end, the bodies of the three missing civil rights workers were found buried in an earthen dam, offering tragic evidence of such violence. My mother and Mr. Jordan were undeterred from fighting their case in court, having failed to convince Virginia politicians like Smith that the poll tax denied their right to vote.

The *Harper and Butts* cases were consolidated, and arguments were scheduled for October 1964 before a three-judge panel in Alexandria. Over the summer, Mr. Jordan reached out to two attorneys, Max Dean and Robert L. Segar of Flint, Michigan, to assist him with the case. Their firm, Leitson, Dean, Dean, Abram and Segar, had been sending its members to the South to work on voter registration cases. They had assisted the National Lawyers Guild with its work, sometimes under dangerous circumstances. Mr. Jordan received a veteran's pension and his wife was a school librarian. The majority of his clients were poor and he did not have a personal fortune to fund his civil rights work. Partnering with Max Dean and Robert Segar ensured that an attorney would continue to litigate for my mother, in the event that Mr. Jordan could not.

Mr. Jordan's amended brief narrowed his constitutional objections to the Fourteenth and Fifteenth amendments. He argued that the poll tax was not a tax to generate revenue, but a device to regulate voting. The Virginia Supreme Court had admitted exactly that in 1939, when it wrote in Campbell v. Goode: "Its imposition was not intended primarily for the production of revenue, but to limit the right of suffrage to those who took sufficient interest in the affairs of the State to qualify themselves to vote." Because the purpose of the poll tax was to hinder Negroes and vast numbers of poor white people from voting, it deprived them of equal protection of the laws. He quoted a 1955 case, *Griffin v. Illinois*, in his brief: "A State can no more discriminate on account of poverty than on account of religion, race or color."

Only property owners received notice of the tax's due date with their regular tax bill, another discrimination against those too poor to own property. Although the revenue from the tax was applied toward free public schools, those schools were still segregated, a condition long ago held unlawful by the U.S. Supreme Court.

The Fifteenth Amendment prohibits discrimination in voting on the basis of race, color, or previous condition of servitude. The constitutional and legislative history of Virginia, and the administration of the poll tax, made clear that disfranchising Negroes was the tax's intent. Jordan surveyed the previous poll tax cases, pointing out that none had raised the issue of discrimination based on economic class.

Harper's complaint was somewhat different from the one Mr. Jordan had written for Mama. Speiser and Brown acknowledged the ratification of the Twenty-fourth Amendment eliminating poll taxes in federal elections. They focused on the Fourteenth Amendment's equal protection clause as justification to invalidate state poll taxes. They also challenged Virginia's constitution and state law for specifically prohibiting "paupers" from registering, even if they were otherwise qualified to vote. This was blatant, indefensible economic discrimination.

During oral arguments that October, Attorney General Robert Button claimed all the plaintiffs lacked standing to challenge the poll tax, specifically because they were paupers, forbidden by Virginia's laws and Constitution from registering in the first place. The judge asked him, "Do you mean every poor person is excluded from registering and could be challenged in Virginia?"

"Yes, sir," Button responded. "I believe exactly what Section 23 of the constitution says." Later he clarified his position further. "My position is that plaintiffs here are not in a position to attack the poll tax as being unconstitutional because they are excluded from voting—because they are paupers."

On November 21, the judges dismissed the plaintiff's Fourteenth Amendment arguments, citing *Breedlove v. Suttles*, which he said had made "arguments akin to those of the plaintiffs here, including the economic factor." The judges were flat-out wrong: As briefs for the plaintiffs had laid out, Nolen Breedlove had not raised the issue of his inability to pay the poll tax because of poverty. The "economic factor" had not been part of that case.

The judges correctly pointed out that none of the plaintiffs had been denied the right to vote because they were paupers. Therefore, they decided, it would be academic for them to render an opinion on the meaning of the word.

The decision was only a momentary setback, for the *Butts and Harper* cases were now bound for the U.S. Supreme Court. The ACLU filed their appeal first. Jordan did not have money to pay the filing fee, so he filed later, and the two cases would again be styled under *Harper v. Virginia State Board of Elections*. Luckily, it takes the Supreme Court a while to accept and schedule a case. If *Harper and Butts* had been heard right away, the court's decision might have been different, owing to its aversion to trumping precedent and its respect for federalism. But, it would take from 1964 to 1966 for the cases to be heard and decided. Momentous changes in the nation were to occur in the interim.

The 1964 presidential campaign was entering its final four months. My mother did her part to make sure the Democratic president won reelection. She worked locally to get out the vote for Johnson, who handily defeated Republican Barry Goldwater—Johnson won 486 electoral votes, while Goldwater carried only his home state of Arizona and five states of the Deep South—Alabama, Georgia, Louisiana, Mississippi, and South Carolina.

Afterwards, Mama probably took a day to recover, then set about organizing a "Sweet Sixteen" birthday party for me, her youngest daughter, and at that point the only child left in the house. The celebration took place at the Phyllis Wheatley YWCA on a Saturday evening. She sewed a special dress for me out of pink brocade, with a daring scooped back featuring a "V" that went down to the waist. She probably stayed up all night to sew the dress. The *Journal and Guide* published a story about the party, listing everyone who attended. It was one of the things my sisters and I loved about our mother—the way she threw herself into both her personal life and public life with total devotion.

In the election's wake, the Southern Christian Leadership Conference and Student Nonviolent Coordinating Committee began to push for expanded federal legislation to ensure voting rights. Johnson instructed U.S. Attorney General Nicholas

Katzenbach to begin working on the issue. Over the ensuing months, the White House and the Justice Department identified three strategies—a constitutional amendment, legislation targeted only at federal elections, or legislation targeted at both state and federal elections. The last option promised to be the most effective, but it would face the toughest fight in Congress. Its success hinged on a thorny question: Was it constitutionally permissible for Congress to ban state poll taxes, when federal poll taxes had been banned by a constitutional amendment?

In January 1965, SCLC and SNCC launched a series of demonstrations in Selma, Alabama, that culminated in violent confrontations with the police. Malcolm X traveled to Selma the following month and gave a militant speech criticizing the nonviolent approach of Martin Luther King. Two days later, President Johnson announced publicly that he would send a voting rights proposal to Congress. Passions ran high. On February 18 in Marion, Alabama, protester Jimmie Lee Jackson, who was unarmed and protecting his mother, was shot and killed by an Alabama state trooper.

Back in Washington, D.C., the Supreme Court was taking a first look at *Harper and Butts* to decide whether to grant the case a plenary hearing or reaffirm Breedlove in a one-line decision. At the February conference, six justices voted in favor of affirming the poll tax. Their thinking was that ratification of the Twenty-fourth Amendment was proof the poll tax was on its way out and there was no need for the Court to act on it. One of the three justices who disagreed was Arthur Goldberg. He wrote an unpublished dissent that is credited with convincing the Court to hear Harper. He cited the long history of legislation to abolish both state and federal poll taxes. All of the bills were proposed because the poll tax clearly violated both the Fourteenth and Fifteenth amendments. The passage of the Twenty-fourth Amendment was not intended to pass judgment on the constitutionality of state poll taxes. It was done to "get some progress in this area." Goldberg's opinion was joined by Chief Justice Warren and Justice William O. Douglas. He circulated it on March 4.

That weekend in Alabama, the protests in Selma reached a shocking climax on the Edmund Pettus Bridge, and March 7, 1965, would forever be remembered as Bloody Sunday. National news organizations filmed footage of unarmed protesters being beaten by state troopers, some on horseback, amid clouds of teargas. The film was flown back to New York City and broadcast that evening to the nation and the world. When the Supreme Court returned to work on Monday, Justices Black, Brennan and White switched sides and voted to grant a hearing to the Virginia poll tax case. Voting rights were simply too important to allow a Depression-era precedent to stand without another long and searching look.

Johnson was determined to turn public outrage over the Selma disgrace into a piece of legislation. The Justice Department was working in overdrive to write a landmark statute on voting rights that would revolutionize the relationship between states and the federal government. The president made a televised speech to Congress on March 15 that might have been the finest of his public life. "What happened in Selma is part of a far larger movement which reaches into every section and state of America," he told his colleagues in government, as well as his countrymen. "It is the effort of American Negroes to secure for themselves the full blessings of American life. Their cause must be our cause, too. Because it is not just Negroes, but really, it's all of us, who must overcome the crippling legacy of bigotry and injustice. And we shall overcome.

"As a man whose roots go deeply into Southern soil I know how agonizing racial feelings are. I know how difficult it is to reshape the attitudes and the structure of our society. But a century has passed, more than a hundred years, since the Negro was freed. And he is not fully free tonight.

"It was more than a hundred years ago that Abraham Lincoln, a great president of another party, signed the Emancipation Proclamation," he said, "but emancipation is a proclamation and not a fact. A century has passed since the day of promise. And the promise is unkept. The time for justice has now come."

My mother watched Johnson make that speech on television in our Norfolk home. She was not the type to cry easily, and she did not cry then. Still, it stunned her to hear a white man from Texas say, "We shall overcome." She had knocked on doors and made phone calls for Johnson, but after that speech, he became her personal president. He won not just her respect, but her heart.

When finally submitted in mid-March, the voting rights legislation included provisions to suspend literacy tests and authorized federal registrars to register blacks for both state and federal elections. Some Southern states were forbidden to change election rules without asking a three-judge panel for permission, to ensure that local officials could not deny rights guaranteed to blacks by the Fifteenth Amendment. No legislation of this nature had been proposed since Reconstruction.

Notably, outlawing state poll taxes was not part of the legislation. When the first hearings were held, Katzenbach testified that he would like to get rid of them, but he was relying on the Supreme Court to do so when it heard the *Harper* case. Not content to wait for the Court, both the House and Senate Judiciary committees added amendments to the bill banning the tax. They were met with filibusters by Southern Democrats that lasted for a month.

At the end of April 1965, the Supreme Court struck down Virginia's attempt to circumvent the Twenty-fourth Amendment by requiring voters to file a certificate of residency to vote in federal elections. The decision offered a ray of hope that the court would overturn Breedlove when it heard Mama's case. "Prior to the proposal of the Twenty-fourth Amendment in 1962," Chief Justice Warren wrote in the opinion, "federal legislation to eliminate poll taxes, either by constitutional amendment or statute, had been introduced in every Congress since 1939. The House of Representatives passed anti-poll tax bills on five occasions and the Senate twice proposed constitutional amendments.

"Even though in 1962 only five States retained the poll tax as a voting requirement, Congress reflected widespread national concern with the characteristics of the tax. Disenchantment with the poll tax was many-faceted. One of the basic objections to the poll tax was that it exacted a price for the privilege of exercising the franchise. Congressional hearings and debates indicate a general repugnance to the disenfranchisement of the poor occasioned by failure to pay the tax."

Despite of the court's opinion, when the filibustering ended the amendments banning state poll taxes were defeated. Instead,

Section 10 of the Voting Rights Act included a declaration by Congress that it found the constitutional rights of citizens to be abridged by poll taxes. Section 10 directed the attorney general, on behalf of the United States, to bring legal actions against any state that required the payment of a poll tax as a precondition to voting.

The Voting Rights Act was passed and signed into law by the president on August 6, 1965. Hundreds of people witnessed his signature, among them Martin Luther King, Rosa Parks, and John Lewis. The Justice Department filed lawsuits against Alabama, Mississippi, Texas, and Virginia.

By statute, the Supreme Court returns to work on the first Monday each October. Presumably, sitting on the justices' desks, or in the hands of their law clerks, was a sixty-seven-page amicus brief in the *Harper* case, filed by the U.S. Department of Justice. It was signed by Attorney General Nicholas Katzenbach, Solicitor General Thurgood Marshall, Assistant Attorney General John Doar, Marshall's assistants Ralph Spritzer and Richard Posner, and Justice attorneys David Rubin, James Kelley and Elihu Leifer.

The brief announced that it would rely on the Fourteenth Amendment to attack the tax. And then it immediately drew attention to Section 10(b) of the Voting Rights Act of 1965, in which Congress instructed the attorney general to institute, "forthwith," proceedings to declare use of the poll tax unconstitutional. "Congress was aware that this case was pending," it argued, "and one of the principal arguments made in favor of a congressional declaration that poll taxes were unconstitutional, rather than an outright prohibition, was the belief that the former approach would avert the likelihood of a remand by this Court."

The United States quoted the recent *Harmen v. Forssenius* decision, which acknowledged that the "original purpose of the Virginia poll tax was to disfranchise Negroes." It agreed with Mr. Jordan's argument that the tax invidiously discriminated against poor persons. But it also argued that there was a more fundamental issue at stake: "That issue (to which our entire brief is devoted) is whether any tax levied on voting, and carrying the sanction of disfranchisement for non-payment, is constitutionally permissible. We urge that it is not." The lawyers argued that it was not necessary to re-examine past poll tax cases because none had posed this fundamental question.

States had made the electoral process the method for determining political questions. If they denied citizens the right to vote, they curtailed political expression, the federal government charged. "The average citizen does not make political speeches, join political clubs, or write letters to newspapers," the brief said. "He expresses himself, in the political arena, only by casting his ballot." The First Amendment's freedoms of political expression, the government concluded, "are not meaningful without a free and fair electoral process."

The United States's argument wielded a bigger and heavier stick than those offered by Mr. Jordan and the ACLU, which relied on the poverty of their plaintiffs and deprivation of their right to equal protection. Congress and the Justice Department had thrown their weight behind the idea that poll taxes of any kind violated the very principles our government was based upon.

It was up to Virginia to argue otherwise. Oral arguments for *Harper* were set for January 25 and 26, 1966. It promised to be much colder than the day Mama went to the March on Washington to hear Martin Luther King speak, but only death could have stopped her from being there.

CHAPTER EIGHT

BEFORE THE COURT

January 25, 1966, was a Tuesday. In those days, the trip from Norfolk to Washington, D.C., was about a five-hour drive. It required, first, crossing the three-mile-long Hampton Roads Bridge-Tunnel from Norfolk to the Virginia Peninsula, then traveling interstate highway west through Williamsburg to Richmond, and north from there to the capital. My parents did not have a car, so my mother got a ride from her friends Alice and Melvin Green. Mrs. Green had relatives in D.C. who put them up for a few nights.

Monday was a clear day for the long drive, but it was cold, and the wind made it feel no more than fifteen degrees. Mr. Jordan also drove to Washington, in a car equipped with hand controls. His wife may have driven or accompanied him. Some details are lost to history.

I wanted to go to Washington. Who wouldn't want to see their mother involved in a case before the United States Supreme Court? I was well aware that nobody, and I mean nobody, had a mother quite like mine. But I was a junior at Norview High, the barely integrated high school near our house, and she did not want me to miss three days of classes. I imagine she was also concerned about staying with Mrs. Green's relatives. She would not have imposed on them by bringing me, too.

I wish we knew so many more details of her trip. In what part of D.C. did they stay? Did they take the bus to the court, or did Mr. Green drive them—and if the latter, where did they park? Where did Mr. Jordan park his car? Did he have difficulty getting his wheelchair into the building and up to the courtroom where oral arguments would be heard?

Once in the courtroom, my mother had the privilege of meeting Thurgood Marshall, whom she had admired since he argued *Brown v. Board of Education* as chief legal counsel for the NAACP. She was surprised to encounter Senator Robert F. Kennedy in the courtroom, too. He had testified against the poll tax to Congress in 1962, when he was attorney general. It was one of the great honors of her life to meet both men. Thankfully, the oral arguments were recorded and have been posted online, so I was able to relive history as though I had been there.

In 1966, there were nine white men on the Supreme Court, ranging in age from forty-nine to eighty. The elders were Hugo Black and William O. Douglas, who'd been appointed by President Roosevelt in the late 1930s. Tom Clark had been appointed by Harry Truman in 1949, and four justices, including the chief justice, had been appointed by President Eisenhower. The court's two most junior justices were Byron White, appointed by President Kennedy, and Abe Fortas, who was serving his first term and had been appointed by President Johnson.

It's been said that Earl Warren was a disappointment to Eisenhower, who expected the former prosecutor, attorney general, and California governor to be a solid conservative voice on the panel. Beginning with the unanimous *Brown* decision desegregating public schools, he'd proved a controversial figure. I remember driving across the country on a family vacation with my sister Jeanette's father-in-law, Raymond Brinkley, his son, and a friend and her daughter in 1963. We kept passing billboards that read, "IMPEACH EARL WARREN" on the way to California, especially in Wyoming and Nevada. I knew he was the chief justice but I had to ask the adults, "Why do they want to impeach him?"

Not surprisingly, the Depression-era justices, Douglas and Black, were born poor and worked their way into the legal field. Both were strong supporters of New Deal legislation and were controversial for different reasons. Black had briefly joined the KKK to advance his political career in Alabama. Douglas, a committed civil libertarian, granted a stay of execution to Ethel and Julius Rosenberg when the court was out of session. It was overturned by the remainder of the justices, and Douglas briefly faced the first of two aborted impeachment proceedings by Congress that would mark his career.

Tom Clark, a Texan, came from a family of lawyers and was the attorney general under President Truman. During World War II, he worked on the forced relocation of Japanese citizens, a program he later criticized. On the court, at times he exercised judicial restraint and at others supported expansionist government. He wrote a 1963 decision declaring Bible reading exercises and mandatory school prayer unconstitutional.

The other three Eisenhower appointees provided the court with two affluent conservatives in John Harlan and Potter Stewart, and one of the panel's most influential liberals in William Brennan. Stewart is perhaps best remembered for writing that he could not define pornography, but "I know it when I see it." Harlan voted for expansion of civil rights on issues like desegregation and interracial marriage, but he voted against requiring police officers to advise arrestees of their constitutional rights in the Miranda case. Brennan was likely appointed to appeal to left-leaning voters during an election year. He was confirmed by the Senate with only Joe McCarthy voting against him.

Byron White and Abe Fortas were too new to the court to characterize in 1966. In addition to being an attorney, White was a professional football player from Colorado who had worked to elect President Kennedy. Abe Fortas was a violin player from a working-class orthodox Jewish family in Tennessee. He taught at Yale Law School, where he became a protégé of William O. Douglas. He'd become friends with Lyndon Johnson in 1939, and nominated Fortas to the seat vacated when Arthur Goldberg was appointed ambassador to the United Nations.

The chief justice opened oral arguments and asked lawyer Allison Brown, representing the *Harper* plaintiffs, to begin. Mr. Brown told the court that their main argument was that a poll tax violated the due process and equal protection clauses of the Fourteenth Amendment. What Mr. Brown was referring to here was the concept of substantive due process, the idea that some rights are fundamental and the government may not take them away without lawful procedures. He explained that the state argued the plaintiffs were paupers and were disqualified by Virginia law from voting, and therefore did not have standing to bring the lawsuit. Being paupers placed them in league with other classes of persons denied the right to vote including "idiots, insane persons, and persons convicted of certain crimes."

However, the District Court had dismissed the plaintiff's case on the authority of the Supreme Court precedent in *Breedlove v. Suttles.* It did not render an opinion on the constitutionality of excluding paupers, as none of the plaintiffs had been denied the right to vote expressly because they were paupers.

Mr. Brown explained that Virginia required residents to pay the tax six months before an election and that persons who had never registered before were required to pay tax for the preceding three years including penalties. This would require a married couple to pay $10.02 to vote. He told the court that 28 percent of Virginians fell below the defined poverty level of $3,000 in annual household income. He clarified that while 22 percent of white Virginians fell below the poverty line, more than half of the state's racial minorities—54 percent of them—did so.

He compared this "invidious" discrimination to that shown in two recent cases, *Griffin v. Illinois and Douglas v. California,* in which the court held that it was unconstitutional to discriminate against the poor. He quoted the opinion of the court in Griffin: "A state can no more discriminate on account of poverty than on account of religion, race or color."

The court asked Mr. Brown to explain the categories of people who were exempt from paying the tax, such as Civil War veterans, their wives or widows, recent veterans, and persons who turned twenty-one after January 1 of the first year they voted. This was not, he pointed out, equal protection under the law.

He next attacked Virginia's contention that the tax represented the most "equal and non-discriminatory test of minimum intelligence and responsibility that could be devised" to determine eligibility for voting. How could payment of a tax be a test of intelligence, he asked—especially when a family member is allowed to pay the tax for a spouse or blood relative?

He reminded the court of recent decisions that held the right to vote could not be taken away by requirements that had no relevance to the state's interest in having an informed electorate and a well-run electoral process. Mr. Brown also argued that rights protected by the First Amendment have little meaning if a citizen did not have the right to vote.

After a recess, he discussed the existence of poll taxes in Vermont, the only northern state that levied them. There, the taxes were required for participation in town meetings, town elections, and school board elections. In sharp contrast to Virginia's discrimination against paupers, Vermont did not require payment from persons who were "actually poor," or persons receiving old-age assistance.

It was at this point that Hugo Black asked Mr. Brown about the Breedlove precedent. Justice Black, eighty years old, had heard the Breedlove case in 1937, his first year on the court. Breedlove had been rendered moot, Mr. Brown told him. In more recent decisions, the court had applied the Fourteenth Amendment to voting rights, and in particular had rendered decisions prohibiting discrimination against the poor.

Justice Black asked him: "You don't think they have to overrule it?"

Mr. Brown replied, stammering: "I think it should be overruled."

The lawyer's audience before the court concluded with a discussion of the District Court's refusal to rule on the constitutionality of excluding "paupers" from registering. He called it a self-enforcing provision, a prior restraint on the exercise of the right to vote. "Any person who considers himself of low economic means and who is aware of his disqualification is simply not going to show up at the polls," he said. "And as long as it stands on the books, it's something that is intolerable." Earl Warren asked if the word had been defined for the purposes of the Act, and Mr. Brown replied that it had not. Warren answered his own question: "They're just people who have very little means."

Now the chief justice called on Thurgood Marshall, the solicitor general, to commence his oral arguments. Mr. Marshall told the court that the United States attached great importance to the issue. He said the poll tax was in full effect only in Alabama, Mississippi, Texas, and Virginia. Because the Voting Rights Act of 1965 removed most of the barriers to voting, the poll tax was now "the one weapon left remaining" to those seeking to quash a minority voice in elections. He explained that Alabama and Mississippi allowed people to register without paying the tax, but they could not actually vote without paying it.

The court asked questions about the amounts of taxes charged in the different states, and whether they required cumulative payment. Mr. Marshall supplied the figures. "The argument, as we see it," he told the justices, "would apply equally if the wealthiest person in Virginia had refused to pay his poll taxes." Simply put, he said, "you cannot put a tax on the right to vote in any form or fashion."

He then made an analogy that would become famous. "While a city can, without question, charge for riding on the municipal subway, and put up a turnstile where you have to put in the fifteen-cent token, I don't believe anybody will try to support a plan where you had to put a dime in a turnstile when you went in to vote.

"It just is completely opposed to any form of democratic government I can think of," he said. Even worse, Virginia required that the tax be paid six months in advance—but only notified those who owned property that they had to pay it.

Potter Stewart noted that the custom of enfranchising property owners rested on the state's desire for voters with a "stake in the government." Mr. Marshall countered that the property requirement existed before public education, and the theory was that a man without property could not afford to send his children to private school. Justice Stewart replied that Marshall's argument was mere theory, and that other theories supported the practice of exacting poll taxes.

Mr. Marshall offered an example illustrating how little the tax signified one's stake in public affairs. A person could refuse to pay $10,000 of taxes in Virginia, and be eligible to vote if he paid the $1.50 poll tax. Was that person a responsible voter? He reiterated the United States' position that payment of a poll tax was not a qualification to vote. He conceded that a poll tax might be a valid tax, but should not be required to vote.

Mr. Marshall and the justices continued to parry on the long history of property ownership as a qualification for voting, and whether a state could show it to be a relevant qualification. Hugo Black said based on history alone, that could be shown. "I would be personally hard pushed to sustain a property qualification, meaning real property," Mr. Marshall told him, "because from age twenty-one until now, I've never owned any real property."

Observers in the courtroom laughed softly. "Now, I don't know how good an elector I am," Mr. Marshall added, "but that's what I see."

Mama and the other onlookers understood only some of what was unfolding before them. It can be difficult for a person not trained in the law to follow the logic of oral arguments; the justices and the lawyers appearing before them are deeply schooled in past cases relevant to the matter at hand, and often refer to them in shorthand—*Breedlove, Thomas, Rash, Terry and Adams, Carrington, Gray and Sanders, Wesberry and Sanders*. To decode this judicial namedropping can force onlookers into the legal section of their local library.

Still, Mama understood enough to admire Mr. Marshall's performance that morning, and she had no trouble following his next line of argument. Mr. Marshall brought up how a recent gerrymandering decision forbade dilution of the vote. He pointed out that dilution of the vote was exactly what the poll tax accomplished.

Byron White asked whether Mr. Marshall's objection to the poll tax as a qualification would apply in a community where everyone was rich. "Absolutely," he answered. Justice White pointed out that his argument was more about due process than equal protection, and Mr. Marshall agreed. William Brennan commented that the argument centered on due process within the rights granted by the First Amendment. Mr. Marshall replied that it said it focused on the same area as freedom of speech and freedom of expression. "It's very little use picketing if you can't vote," he said.

In concluding, Mr. Marshall said the United States strongly urged the court to declare poll taxes unconstitutional, so that people who had recently registered after passage of the Voting Rights Act would be able to vote in the fall elections without hindrance.

Now it was time for my mother's case to be argued. She was the only plaintiff present in the courtroom. In fact, Mr. Jordan had heard from the ACLU attorneys that the *Harper* plaintiffs were afraid of repercussions against them for challenging the state of Virginia. They regretted becoming involved in the lawsuit, and would have preferred to withdraw. Though Fairfax County was closer to Washington, D.C., they stayed away from oral arguments on those cold, windy days, which is how the Associated Press wound up photographing my mother alone in front of the Supreme Court.

Robert Segar, one of Mr. Jordan's co-counsels from Flint, Michigan, spoke on Mama's behalf. The distinguishing thing about Mr. Segar's exchange with the court is that Justice Black pushed back harder on him than he had on Thurgood Marshall, telling Mr. Segar: "I don't quite get the relevance here of the statistics about how much money people have." Justice Black questioned why Congress did not outlaw poll taxes by legislation. He asked Mr. Segar if he thought Congress had the right to abolish poll taxes, as it had abolished literacy tests. Mr. Segar stammered a little bit in affirming that he thought Congress could do that, but such legislation might be dubious.

Justice Black pressed him. "You mean that the court could do it even though the Congress couldn't?"

Mr. Segar replied: "I think that's exactly right."

Some discussion followed on whether the Twenty-fourth Amendment and Voting Rights Act was relevant to the case. Mr. Segar told the justices that Mama's case was filed before either became law, and did not rely on either for its argument against the poll tax.

He devoted his concluding remarks to First Amendment arguments. "One of the most precious rights in a free society is that of having a voice in the election of those officials who make the laws under which we as good citizens must live," he said. "Other rights, even the most basic, are illusory if the right to vote is undermined." He asked that the remainder of his time be reserved until later, so that Mr. Jordan could speak.

In the meantime, it was finally the Commonwealth of Virginia's turn to defend its poll tax. The state's case was argued by George D. Gibson, an attorney from Richmond. One can know nothing about Mr. Gibson, but listening to the session tapes it becomes obvious that he hailed from a privileged background— at least, if it's fair to infer that from his almost Etonesque eloquence, his accent—which wasn't the least bit Southern—and his confidence before the justices. This didn't necessarily work to his advantage: All but two justices, Stewart and Harlan, had humble beginnings.

Mr. Gibson acknowledged the plaintiffs' desire to enlarge their opportunities, but he said it should be done "through lawful means." He made plain that Virginia viewed the poll tax as an issue of state's rights, telling the court: "Individual freedom is not likely to survive, unless the court also respects the federalist principle which was the great means by which a union of many states was formed and has been maintained." Virginia's argument would elevate the text of the Constitution giving states the right to set qualifications for electors above any amendments regarding due process, equal protection, or freedom of expression.

He airily brushed aside the plaintiffs' complaints about the burden of paying the poll tax six months in advance. "All that is necessary in order to satisfy the requirements of the poll tax is, you pay $1.50 in each year by December 5," he said. He told Justice Black that he should have the "comfort of approaching with complete serenity" the absence of constitutional questions presented in oral arguments, that only a "few statistics from census" were offered. It is difficult not to read these comments as an insult to the appellants' attorneys and the solicitor general representing the United States.

Mr. Gibson told the court that oral arguments had "simplified" the issues presented. His "learned brother Brown" had admitted that *Breedlove v. Suttles* was controlling, and needed to be overruled. The solicitor general had abandoned the arguments made in his briefs to argue that voting rights stemmed from the First Amendment, "alluding to his argument but without any consistency." And he said that his "Brother Segar" had admitted that Virginia's motives for adopting the poll tax were not determinative. What mattered was the operation of the law.

"If anything can be accepted as a certainty, it's this," he told the court. "That in adopting the Constitution in 1788, no colonial state imagined, for a moment, that it was thereby relinquishing its sovereign authority to establish the qualifications, the suffrage, in his own local elections." When election of senators was transferred from the Electoral College to a popular vote in 1913, states retained the right to set qualifications for electors.

Mr. Gibson attacked the idea that voting rights were related to freedom of expression, by stating that if the First Amendment had guaranteed voting rights, there would have been no need for the Fifteenth, Nineteenth and Twenty-fourth amendments. He reminded the justices that states adopted the Fourteenth Amendment, guaranteeing equal protection under the law, circa 1868, and that its second section provided that reducing the number of males eligible to vote would reduce the state's representation in Congress. The amendment gave no powers to Congress to curtail a state's right to set qualifications for voting, so he found it novel that the appellants' attorney would use it in their arguments against the poll tax. He also mentioned that when the amendment was ratified, ten of the twenty-three ratifying states required property or other tax payments in order to vote, including Massachusetts.

The Fifteenth and Nineteenth amendments narrowly prohibited discrimination on account of race or sex, Mr. Gibson said. He reminded the court that both the Senate and House Judiciary committees were assured that the Twenty-fourth Amendment would "not prevent the imposition of a poll tax as a prerequisite for voting in state or local elections." Nothing in the history of the Constitution or its amendments could suggest anything other than states had the right to set qualifications for voting.

Mr. Gibson next tackled voting cases decided by the Supreme Court. He mentioned Pope v. Williams, a 1904 decision that allowed states to require electors to register a year in advance—and thus decreed that the privilege to vote in any state was not given by the U.S. Constitution. He couldn't resist another jab at Thurgood Marshall: "No wonder my learned brother now has difficulty in identifying the [constitutional] provision on which they rest." He claimed the court's Guinn decision of 1915 "pointed out that the Fifteenth Amendment did not take away state authority over suffrage because it had belonged to the state governments from the beginning."

In discussing the Fourteenth Amendment, Abe Fortas asked him a direct question. "If I understand your position, then," the justice said, "you do not regard the right to vote as within any part of the Fourteenth Amendment—either the Privileges and Immunities Clause, or the Equal Protection Clause."

"Yes, Mr. Justice Fortas," Gibson replied, "that's quite correct."

Justice Fortas asked him to set aside the Fifteenth Amendment for a moment. Was there anything in the Constitution that would prevent a state from saying that no Negroes could vote? Gibson answered that without the Fifteenth Amendment, it would be legal to deny Negroes the right to cast a ballot.

Mr. Gibson claimed that Virginia's poll tax did not discriminate. He quoted the U.S. Civil Rights Commission's 1959 finding that the tax was not the serious restriction it once had been. Yes, he said, the Virginia constitutional convention of 1902 had sought to eliminate the illiterate from voting. But he reminded the justices that the state's motivation was irrelevant, anyway—it was not grounds for invalidating legislation. As he was beginning to take up the issue of the relationship between a poll tax and the actual qualification of voters to cast a ballot, the chief justice called a recess for the day.

The two justices who had asked the most questions were Hugo Black and Byron White—the longest-serving justice and the second newest. There was no doubt that Justice Black was not on Mama's side. The opinion in the case would be written by his good friend and fellow Depression-era nominee, William O. Douglas, but Douglas had posed very few questions in that first day before the court, mostly asking for clarification on facts such as which four states still had a poll tax. His demeanor gave no clue as to his thoughts on the issue before him.

After her long day in the courtroom, I am sure my mother's head was in a spin. She had listened to Mr. Brown, Mr. Marshall and Mr. Segar argue about the historical origins of the poll tax as a vehicle to prevent black people from voting. She'd heard them describe the tax's effect on poor people, and its magnified effect on poor black people. She'd heard them characterize the tax as a curtailment of the rights to equal protection of the law, due process and freedom of expression. She'd listened as Mr. Marshall argued that charging people to vote was undemocratic on its face. All these arguments were about assuring that everyone had the same rights—rights guaranteed by the Constitution. All held that discrimination against the poor was indefensible. Mr. Marshall had emphasized, further, that Congress wanted the poll tax abolished, and had said as much in the Voting Rights Act. And federal poll taxes had been abolished by the Twenty-fourth Amendment, which should signal that poll taxes were simply not fair. When the attorneys had finished their arguments, she'd had no doubts that they were right, that state poll taxes were unconstitutional, and that she would prevail.

But then Mr. Gibson had argued about rules, rather than rights. If the Constitution said that states had the right to set qualifications for voting, he saw no room for them to be abolished except by the states. He flatly denied that there was anything unfair in the administration of collecting poll taxes, even though very few Negroes were registered in Virginia. He made excuses for the state's constitutional convention of 1902, ignoring the speeches of those who blatantly admitted poll taxes were intended to disfranchise Negroes. He insulted Mr. Marshall's argument that without the right to vote, the First Amendment was meaningless. He even said that without the Fifteenth Amendment, it was legal to deny black people the right to vote!

This was why it was so frustrating to live in the South. White people would never admit when they were wrong. Sometimes, it seemed as though the Supreme Court justices were deferential to Mr. Gibson, rather than the other way around. She had a bad feeling at the end of the day that rules might have more weight than rights.

I imagine Mr. Jordan would have comforted her a little. This is what lawyers do in court, he'd have told her—they attack each other's arguments. She should not take personally that Mr. Gibson had been so forceful with Mr. Marshall, because they were in a verbal duel and only one side would win. Maybe Gibson attacked him so hard because he feared the moral force of his argument.

I think the Associated Press photograph might have been shot just after they left the courtroom, because the next day there would be a light snow and fog in Washington, D.C., and I don't see any evidence that it's snowing in the picture. I can also see by the expression on my mother's face that she was determined and resolute, but she was not smiling. She looked far from relaxed, as though the battle's outcome was uncertain.

My mother and the Greens would have returned to their hosts' home for dinner. I don't know whether the Jordans joined them. I hope they did. I hope all of them joined in good food and good conversation. I hope the weight of the day's events was not heavy on their moods, and that they laughed. I wonder where everybody slept. Did Mrs. Green's relatives have a spare bedroom? Did they double up on beds and the living room sofa? I don't know these details, but this I do know: My mother may not have had much in material possessions, but she enjoyed the luxury of deep friendships with women like Alice Green, who'd made sure she had a ride to Washington and a place to sleep for a few nights. Who'd ensured she could play a part in history.

The next day, Mr. Gibson came fast out of the gate, reading from congressional testimony given by Attorney General Nicholas Katzenbach. He quoted Mr. Katzenbach telling the House Judiciary Committee that it would be difficult to abolish poll taxes under the Fifteenth Amendment, based on the fact that they had been used to discriminate.

Before the Senate Judiciary Committee, he'd been asked: "Under the Fourteenth Amendment, you think Congress has the right by statute to eliminate the poll tax and I hear you say that in your opinion?"

"No, senator," Mr. Katzenbach had replied. "I do not think they do." He explained that the Supreme Court had held in the past that poll taxes did not violate the Fourteenth Amendment, but it was going to reexamine the question.

Mr. Gibson then attacked the idea that paying a $1.50 fixed tax was too great a burden for the appellants or anyone. He argued that the amount was so "insubstantial as to merit dismissal on that ground alone." Three or four times more poor whites were subject to the tax than poor blacks, he pointed out—which diminished the argument that the tax violated the Fifteenth Amendment, which prohibits denial of voting rights based on race.

Justice Fortas referred to Mr. Gibson's comments of the previous day, when he'd said that a state's power to fix the qualifications of voters was "not limited by questions of reasonableness or any other questions." Mr. Gibson elaborated. "My basic premise," he now told the justices, "is that the right to vote in state elections is a state-created right, and may be given or withheld on such terms and conditions as the state may determine." This line of thinking raised the possibility that a state might charge a poll tax of far more than $1.50 per year.

Mr. Gibson then reiterated Virginia's argument that payment of a fixed tax six months in advance was a non-discriminatory way to ensure that the most informed and responsible voters would present themselves at the polls. The chief justice brought up Mr. Marshall's argument about the rich person who ducks paying thousands of dollars in tax, but does pay the $1.50 poll tax. Mr. Gibson deflected, saying, "It's designed not as a financial requirement nor an overall test of civic virtue, but rather as an index of minimum competence—and only that."

Justice Fortas once again brought Mr. Gibson back to his beliefs about a state's power to set qualifications for voters. Admitting that it was an absurd hypothetical, but one that would help clarify the issue, he asked whether a state could allow only redheads to vote. Mr. Gibson declined to give any serious answer, but reiterated his point: "My submission to the court is that the state power is unequivocal and unlimited." Looking back on it more than fifty years later, this might have been the moment that sealed Mr. Gibson's fate, along with the commonwealth's, and consigned poll taxes to the dustbin of history. Justice Fortas thanked him for his answer, indicating that he now fully understood his thinking.

Mr. Gibson's closing comments brought the court back to its Breedlove and Butler decisions, which had affirmed poll taxes. Nothing had changed, he said, since the justices had decided those cases. He made a last sally that poll taxes were a "familiar, historical, well-known, and widely used legislative pattern." And he looped his argument back to the first point he'd made the day before: "We submit, therefore, that the judgment below should be affirmed for no technical or trivial reason, but to fulfill in all phases, the great mandate of the Constitution for a division of authority between the central and the state government, which is the mainspring of the creation and endurance of our federal system."

Mr. Brown rose to clarify a point discussed the day before. In Virginia, local, state and federal elections could be held at different times. Justice White asked him if his position on the poll tax was based solely on the Fourteenth Amendment. He said it was—its clauses guaranteeing both due process and equal protection. He cautioned the court that to "take a rigid view of Article 1, Section 2, and say that the right to vote flows only from the states—and exists only by the grace of the states—it seems to us, is to do an injustice to our democracy." He added: "A democratic form of government, as every school child knows, means that a person has a right to vote."

Justice Black then asked a strange theoretical question: Could a state decide to appoint all of its officers? Mr. Brown immediately responded that it would violate Article 4, Section 4 of the Constitution, which guarantees a republican form of government. That section, called the Guarantee Clause, reads: "The United States shall guarantee to every state in this union a republican form of government, and shall protect each of them against invasion; and on application of the legislature, or of the executive (when the legislature cannot be convened) against domestic violence."

Justice Black pointed out that people are appointed to work in agencies, and that senators used to be elected by state legislators, not voters. He asked if it was up to the court to decide what a "republican form of government" actually meant. Mr. Brown brought the discussion back from the theoretical to the case at hand, saying that the court had found rights in the First Amendment that were not explicitly mentioned there—the rights to privacy, to travel, to earn a living. Justice Black asked him whether he wanted the court to read the right to vote into the First Amendment. Mr. Brown said that yes, he did.

He began his concluding argument by quoting the court that without the right to vote, other rights the citizens have are illusory—that those rights could be taken away by persons over whom they have no control. He urged the court to refute the notion that the right to vote derives only from the states, and to find that it resides in the protections afforded by the First Amendment.

Finally, it was time for Mr. Jordan to speak. Normally, an attorney argues from a lectern in the center of the room, in front of the bench. I wonder what effect it had on the court to see him roll his wheelchair up to the lectern. I wonder whether the justices knew that he'd been wounded in the war. How long did it take for him to adjust the microphone? Did he have help?

Mr. Jordan was a tenor with the slightest of Southern accents, and he spoke slowly and deliberately. He began with an understatement: "We have been privileged, on yesterday, and on today, for quite a lesson in history from the appellee." Then he abandoned understatement for hyperbole. "If we take that lesson as it was given, I believe we would have to conclude that Mrs. Butts, the appellant, and all those of like racial hue, were suddenly unemancipated."

Mr. Gibson's history lesson had been corrupted, he said. "What we have heard has been a lesson in state's rights—a state's rights to take away, but no comment upon the state's responsibility to its citizens," he told the justices. "We submit that the intent of the convention of 1902 was to disfranchise the Negroes as a group. And we say to you that places a different light upon what has been accomplished. Because following the convention and the implementation of the poll tax laws which had passed, the exact evil which it intended has been accomplished."

Before the 1902 convention, Mr. Jordan told the court, Negroes held numerous seats in Virginia's General Assembly. "Almost like a magic wand, after the passage of . . . these poll tax laws, not a single Negro has sat in the Virginia General Assembly, and not a single Negro has held a single elected state office in the state of Virginia. We say that the evil intent was accomplished, and that it was accomplished in direct confrontation to the Fifteenth Amendment."

He acknowledged that the appellees claimed the law was administered fairly, but he questioned how that was possible. Every time a poll tax statement was made, every time a poll tax was collected, and every time a list of registered voters was written, it was furthering the discrimination brought about by the 1902 convention. He cited the state's own figures: that 78,000 Negroes earned between $1,000 and $1,900 per year; that 139,000 earned less than $1,000 per year; and that 106,000 Negroes earned nothing at all. All these people suffered discrimination as a direct result of the 1902 convention, he said. My mother, the appellant, had been denied rights guaranteed to her by the Fifteenth Amendment, but as she was also denied the right to petition the government, that discrimination had "mushroomed" to include her First Amendment rights.

The last words recorded during oral arguments were Mr. Jordan's. "What Virginia accomplished by its action in 1902 was to create two body politics in Virginia, a white body politic and a Negro body politic," he told the justices. "The Negroes have been effectively eliminated from any political power in Virginia—eliminated and separated from the political power which is now exercised by the whites exclusively, to the exclusion of Negroes."

And then the tape of oral arguments cuts off. It seems as though there must have been more. Did the Justices have questions for Mr. Jordan? Did he thank them when he finished? Would he have ended abruptly without arguing that the poll tax violated the Fourteenth Amendment? Right now, as I write this, I don't know the answers to these questions, so there remains more digging to be done.

My mother and Mr. and Mrs. Green drove back to Norfolk right after oral arguments concluded that second day, arriving home after dark. When she stepped through the door, she told us she had met Bobby Kennedy and Thurgood Marshall in person. Our news for her was that her picture had appeared on the front page of *The Virginian-Pilot* that morning. My father or my mother's friends probably saved multiple copies for her. I'm sure the phone rang off the hook the next day, with people asking her questions about her day in the high court.

I know for a fact that the Supreme Court justices held a conference on January 28, at which they took a vote. I know this because William O. Douglas's papers are housed in the Library of Congress for anyone to read. In his sloppy, almost indecipherable handwriting, he wrote down their initial decisions on a single page with a blue pen:

CJ reverses—rests on Equal Protection tho First Amend argument is valid—this is a discrimination against poor + against Negroes on a fact—Breedlove could be [?]

HLB takes other view—affirms—poll tax is a tax that was first to discriminate against race—Congress can ban it— then Ct [?] not usurp Congress because of its views on social policy—does not agree with Va's argument at Bar— states were left with favor to regulate elections

WOD—reverses

TC reverses—it is [?] discrimination

JMH affirms

WJB reverses

FEARLESS

PS affirms

BW reverses

AF   "

The decision would be 6-3 to reverse Breedlove. My mother and the *Harper* plaintiffs and the people of the United States won the day. I should note that justices Douglas and Black were quite fond of each other—they had served on the court together since 1939, and often concurred with each other's opinions. Not this time.

Remember, too, that Arthur Goldberg was no longer on the court. He'd written the memo a year earlier that convinced his fellow justices to hear the *Harper* case and reconsider Breedlove. The justices might not be competitive with each other, but they are certainly aware of each other's work. Justice Douglas had just written the majority decision in the 1965 contraception case, Griswold v. Connecticut, which found a right to privacy in the First Amendment, penning a phrase which would become famous: "Specific guarantees in the Bill of Rights have penumbras, formed by emanations from those guarantees that help give them life and substance." Justice Black dissented in Griswold. But it was Justice Goldberg who earned attention for his concurring opinion in Griswold, which found for the plaintiff based solely on the Ninth Amendment—"The enumeration in the Constitution, of certain rights, shall not be construed to deny or disparage others retained by the people." Undoubtedly, Justice Douglas took all of this into consideration as he wrote approximately thirty drafts of his opinion in the poll tax cases.

In H*arper and Butts*, the Court was presented with numerous amendments to consider—the First, Thirteenth, Fourteenth and Fifteenth. The Court was also alerted to Section 10 of the Voting Rights Act, in which Congress declared poll taxes unconstitutional and directed the Department of Justice to file lawsuits against the remaining states that levied them. The United States brief also referred to the recent passage of the Twenty-fourth Amendment outlawing federal poll taxes. After oral arguments, lower federal courts declared poll taxes unconstitutional, in Texas on February 9, and in Alabama on March 3. But, when Justice Douglas's opinion was released on March 24, 1966, it focused solely on the Fourteenth Amendment, not even mentioning the Voting Rights Act or the Twenty-fourth Amendment, though he did acknowledge the Texas and Alabama court decisions in footnotes.

He opened the opinion by stating a conundrum. The right to vote in federal elections is conferred by Article 1, Section 2 of the Constitution. The right to vote in state elections is nowhere expressly mentioned, but implied. "We do not stop to canvass the relation between voting and political expression," he wrote. In other words, arguments based on the First Amendment were so obvious as to be unnecessary. However, he continued, "once the franchise is granted to the electorate, lines may not be drawn which are inconsistent with the Equal Protection Clause of the Fourteenth Amendment." That is to say, the right of suffrage "is subject to the imposition of state standards which are not discriminatory and which do not contravene any restriction that Congress. . . has imposed."

He left no doubt that the Constitution itself forbade state poll taxes, writing: "We conclude that a State violates the Equal

Protection Clause of the Fourteenth Amendment whenever it makes the affluence of the voter or payment of any fee an electoral standard." He dispensed with Virginia's argument that the poll tax was simply a time-honored method for selecting electors who were invested in voting and had proven themselves responsible. "We must remember that the interest of the State, when it comes to voting, is limited to the power to fix qualifications," he wrote. "Wealth, like race, creed, or color, is not germane to one's ability to participate intelligently in the electoral process."

Justice Douglas then went on to give the court permission to apply the Fourteenth Amendment to areas where it had previously refrained from extending it. "The Equal Protection Clause is not shackled to the political theory of a particular era," he wrote. "Notions of what constitutes equal treatment for purposes of the Equal Protection Clause do change. This Court, in 1896, held that laws providing for separate public facilities for white and Negro citizens did not deprive the latter of equal protection and treatment that the Fourteenth Amendment commands."

The court had overturned that precedent in the past, Justice Douglas wrote, and it was now overturning Breedlove. From that time forward, my mother referred to William O. Douglas as "my justice." She adopted him as her own, as she had Lyndon Johnson.

Justice Black dissented, as did justices Harlan and Stewart. Justice Black's dissent acknowledged that Breedlove was decided a few weeks after he took his seat on the court in 1937. His dissent was based on his belief that state poll taxes should be abolished through a constitutional amendment, and not by expanding the scope of the existing Fourteenth Amendment. "I can only conclude," he wrote, "that the primary, controlling, predominant, if not the exclusive, reason for declaring the Virginia law unconstitutional is the Court's deep-seated hostility and antagonism, which I share, to making payment of a tax a prerequisite to voting." In other words, Justice Black was on Mama's side in spirit, but not in method.

The Virginian-Pilot ran a story the next day under the headline, "Va. Poll Tax Killed by Court." The reporter called Mr. Jordan a "champion of lost causes," writing: "The victory has special significance for Jordan, who has failed in several other civic causes." At the end of the story, he enumerated Mr. Jordan's failures for several paragraphs. "This matter of the poll tax, I guess, has been with me all of my life," Mr. Jordan was quoted as saying. "My father pointed it out to me as the key thing on which we could build a better state."

My mother was pragmatic in her comments to the paper. "I think the impact will just be that we will have more registered voters," she told the reporter, predicting that it would translate into "better treatment" for potential Negro voters.

After the decision, my mother set about registering voters— thousands of them, along with her friends and associates in the Women of Virginia's Third Force. As the group's president, Mama was credited with registering more voters in Virginia than any other individual.

Victory in the poll tax case earned my mother the right to vote, free of restrictions. It also got her a new kitchen appliance. To mark the decision's first anniversary, the Oakwood Rosemont Civic League held a banquet to honor Mama, and the members gave her a modern new refrigerator. Her friends and neighbors knew that the door on our old refrigerator had to be propped up with a big stick to stay shut. The new fridge served as a monument to my mother's belief that no injustice was too hard to fight—and that with victory, great and small rewards would follow.

CHAPTER NINE

FOUR LESSONS

In the first chapter, I said that I hoped this book would be a blueprint for today's activists so they may follow in my mother's footsteps to become influential figures in local politics, and not be deterred by poverty or social status or competition.

The first lesson to take from the life of Evelyn Butts is that you cannot do anything alone. You must get out of the house and join or create a group of like-minded individuals who will work toward the same goals. My mother belonged to many groups. One of the most important was the Women of Virginia's Third Force. The name is somewhat misleading—it was not some ladies' auxiliary. There was no group called Men of Virginia's Third Force. The women did almost all the work.

Mr. Jordan had always said that the mass of eligible unregistered voters was a third force that could change Virginia's politics. He was right. After the poll tax case, my mother and her friends and associates in the Third Force came up with a plan to find and register those voters in the black community. Using the handwritten list my mother had compiled after attorneys Holt and Dawley sued to inspect the voter registration rolls, the women registered 3,000 voters in a six-month period.

This accomplishment is all the more remarkable because each of those voters had to go to the election office to register in person. The Third Force bought advertisements in the paper offering rides to people who did not have cars. They worked with ministers to encourage congregations to register. The city registrar expanded office hours to accommodate the demand for voter registration. With time and pressure, the rules were changed so that voter registration drives could be conducted away from the election office.

The Third Force women who worked with Mama were Charlotte Ambrose, Martha Balmer, Margaret Bly, Alease Brickers, Willie Mae Bridges, Anna Lee Brinkley, Parthenia Britt, Pauline Britt, Minnie Brownson, Sally Coe, Effie Conley, Ruby Cooke, Alberta Eason, Josie Gazell, Melsie Giddens, Agnes Gould, Beatrice Grace, Alice Green, Alveta Green, Lula Gwaltney, Thelma Harris, Pauline Hart, Maggie Hines, Leona W Holt, Pearlene Jackson, Mary Jackson, Annie Jackson, Maria Jenkins, Janie C Jordan, Delores B Jordan, Agnes Jordan, Queen Joyner, Annie Lamb, Lady Manning, Vivian C Mason, Mozelle Mitchell, Mary Myers, Annie Nickens, Bertha Parker, Alverta Pegram, Amy Phinazaa, Pearl Robinson, Harriett Selden, Annie Mae Simons, Mary Smith, Alberta Smith, Gertrude Sullivan, Frances Taylor, Minnie B Ward, Georgia Warren, Georgia M Warren, Octavia Wescott, Fannie White, Rebecca Williams, Johnny Wilson, Louise Winfield, Louberta Woody, and Marie Young. There were undoubtedly more, but the historical records for this group consist of old photos and newspaper articles. I wish I had a complete list. The men who belonged to the Third Force whose names I can remember were Walter Green, Tom Graves, Melvin Green, and J.D. Speller.

The women had a greater goal in mind. They registered black voters to elect black candidates. Mama belonged to, and was later chairwoman of, the Concerned Citizens for Political Education, a grass-roots organization centered on Norfolk's east side that had evolved out of others. After the city's African Americans fell short in their efforts to elect blacks to office in the 1950s and early 1960s, they'd formed a group called the Committee of Forty to register voters and endorse candidates. The Committee of Forty morphed into the Citizens United for Responsible Government, which was later reconstituted as the Concerned Citizens. All of these organizations had in common a simple but powerful tool that they wielded as election day approached: They distributed a sample ballot on yellow paper, in a shade the printing industry knows as goldenrod.

The "Goldenrod Ballot" became an immensely influential feature of Norfolk elections. A black or white politician winning the Concerned Citizens' endorsement, and thus earning a place on that sheet of paper, was all but guaranteed to win 90 percent of the black vote. And that was enough to decide many contests: By the late 1960s, blacks represented 35 percent of the city's registered voters. A white candidate who shared the white vote with his or her rivals, but won the black vote, soon had "the honorable" in front of his name. On the other hand, any political hopeful spurning that bloc, black or white, had to capture an outsized share of Norfolk's white vote to prevail at the polls.

The city's electoral structure worked for and against black influence. In contests for the seven-member Norfolk City Council, three spots might be up for grabs at once, and all represented the entire city, and gained office in a city-wide vote. Norfolk was not, in other words, divided into wards, each with its own representative; all on the council theoretically spoke for every neighborhood, every voter, every persuasion and race.

Black voters were outnumbered by their white counterparts by a two-to-one margin, which on its face was a tremendous hurdle. But with the help and guidance of the Concerned Citizens, they learned to maximize their influence. A black voter entering the polling booth could "single shot" his vote, and vote for only a single black candidate on the ballot. This assured that candidate received the bulk of the black community's vote—and just as importantly, denied that vote to everyone else—and gave him or her a strong place among everyone running. If a slew of white candidates were seeking office, as was sometimes the case, they might theoretically split the white vote so that a strong black candidate with his or her 30-something percent topped them.

The black voter could, conversely, vote for three candidates— that was certainly his or her right—but that diluted the effects of his ballot. Both the Goldenrod ballot and single-shot voting became controversial topics as the community began to strategize how to best utilize its new voting power.

The second and most obvious lesson from my mother's life is that you must put in the time if you want to be successful in politics, and be willing to do the most mundane things.

As I mentioned before, Mr. Jordan had run for the General Assembly in 1959 as a write-in candidate, and had lost. He'd been on the ballot in the Norfolk City Council election of 1960, and had lost again. During the city council race, my mother had enlisted me and a dozen other teenage girls to bring attention to his campaign. She named us the Jordanettes. We wore matching dresses that my mother sewed in three different colors—red, white or navy blue. The white dress was sleeveless, and the red and blue dresses, short-sleeved. Mama sewed all the dresses for all the girls, taking about three hours to cut, pin and sew each. Afterward, each of the Jordanettes came to our house for a fitting. Each of us had one of each color, meaning that Mama created thirty-six dresses—and at three hours each, spent at least 108 hours on the project, the equivalent of two-and-a-half full-time work weeks.

One of Mr. Jordan's supporters, Peter Babalas, was a white state senator. The Jordanettes passed out literature at a fundraiser that he hosted at his house. The crowd was mostly white. We put pro-Jordan bumper stickers on every car without asking permission. When I told Mama, she said, "Oh. I don't know if that was a good thing." I asked if we were going to get in trouble. She chuckled and assured me, "If they don't like it, they can take it off." The Jordanettes became the Spellerettes in 1966, when we worked for J.D. Speller, a black labor leader who ran for city council. He lost, too.

There was a group of liberal white people in Norfolk who believed the time had come to elect blacks to office. Some scholars of the city's history refer to this group as the "silkstockings," because they were wealthy and well-educated. Many of its members belonged to the business community, which had publicly opposed Massive Resistance.

In 1967, Henry Howell, a populist politician who was determined to offer an alternative to the Byrd Machine, ran for the

Virginia Senate. At the same time, a slate for House of Delegates, calling itself the "Norfolk First" ticket, included a black candidate, William P. Robinson, a professor of political science at Norfolk State College. While this represented progress, certainly some in the black community felt that white power brokers were offering up a black candidate who was acceptable, or "safe," to them. Mr. Jordan was among the critics, and announced his candidacy for House of Delegates on the same day the Norfolk First ticket unveiled its slate.

The race pitted the two men against each other in a bitter contest. Norfolk's Democratic Party endorsed Mr. Robinson. Mr. Jordan had the Concerned Citizens' backing. But predictably, the two split the black vote, which doomed them in the contest. Neither candidate won.

The two decided never to let outsiders pit them against each other again. They agreed that Mr. Jordan would run for Norfolk City Council in 1968, and that Mr. Robinson would run again for the House of Delegates in 1969, thereby ensuring that both would be endorsed by the Concerned Citizens. The strategy worked: Mr. Jordan was elected in 1968, and for the first time in the twentieth century, Virginia had a black elected official.

National events cast a pall over this local victory. On April 4, 1968, Martin Luther King was assassinated in Memphis, Tennessee. I remember when the news flashed on the television. I was twenty years old, already married, and the mother of one child. I just happened to stop by Mama's house. That day marked the first time I saw my mother cry. No amount of personal tragedy had moved her to cry in front of her children. That day, we cried together. Hers were tears of anger, as well as heartache: She was furious that anyone would take King's life when his movement was non-violent.

In November 1966, Dr. King had come to Norfolk to speak at New Calvary Baptist Church during the installation of its new pastor. Mama had met him during that visit. I wish we'd recorded her recollections of meeting him. I know she'd been introduced to him as the plaintiff who brought an end to Southern poll taxes, and that eliminating state poll taxes had been among his highest political priorities. Throughout the negotiations over the Voting Rights Act, he had consistently pressed the attorney general, senators and congressmen about the chilling effects of those state-level taxes. Following the elimination of federal poll taxes fell in 1964 and the passage of the Voting Rights Act in 1965, those taxes had loomed as a last vestige of racial vote-quashing. From all indications, Dr. King had been jubilant to meet my mother, the plaintiff who accomplished his dream of ending state poll taxes. She had not asked to have her photograph taken with him, and I think she regretted that for the rest of her life.

Two days after the assassination she was scheduled to work at Stein's, a men's clothing store on Granby Street. Easter was a couple of weeks away, and the store's owners needed extra help with alterations and hemming trouser cuffs. Mama put on all the Martin Luther King buttons she could find and went to work. She could not stop talking about the assassination. Not only was she angry at the person or persons who had shot King, she abhorred the rioting that had erupted in urban centers around the country in the assassination's wake. She believed deeply in nonviolence, and she saw rioting as a slap in King's face, an insult to his memory. When she left the store, she realized that the managers at Stein's had been uncomfortable with her anger. Sure enough, they did not ask her to come back for the Christmas season. Mr. Jordan proposed to the Norfolk City Council two years later that a memorial to the slain civil rights leader be erected in the city. The idea was not supported. Five years later, when Mr. Jordan was Vice-Mayor, the proposal passed on a 5-2 vote. Councilman Claude Staylor, a former Norfolk police chief, opposed the monument. He compared King to Angela Davis, H. Rap Brown, Eldridge Cleaver, and Stokely Carmichael, stating that he shared J.Edgar Hoover's "disdain for him".

In May 1968, the national Poor People's Campaign marched through Norfolk. May is a beautiful month in Norfolk. Azaleas, crape myrtles, and every other flower, it seems, is in bloom, and the summer's coming furnace heat has not yet arrived. The wounds from the assassination were still raw as 1,000 marchers arrived in buses on their way to Washington, D.C., where they planned to camp on the National Mall and protest in front of federal agencies. The Poor People's Campaign went to Norfolk City Hall and presented a petition of grievances to the city's leaders, including the need for jobs, an end to job discrimination, free medical and dental care for families earning less than $100 a week, a massive building program, and the passage of an open housing ordinance by the city council. A "tell-it-like-it-is" rally was held at Foreman Field, the stadium at Old Dominion University, that night. Music and speeches inspired the crowd of 2,500.

The stopover in Norfolk included workshops on how to take militant action without damage to property or people. In the wake of the riots after King's assassination, SCLC wanted to reconfirm its commitment to nonviolence. The marchers were housed in people's homes all over the city, and Mama's house was among them. She and her friend Alveta each had room for one person. Alveta fed breakfast cereal to her guest, and drove to our house to pick up Mama's lodger. There they discovered that Mama had made enough breakfast to feed a half-dozen people—eggs, biscuits, sausage, hash browns. "You're making me look bad," Alveta told her. "I just fed mine cereal." Everybody lingered at Mama's house to finish her lavish breakfast before heading downtown.

Incredibly, the following month, Robert F. Kennedy was shot in Los Angeles while campaigning for president. I don't know whether today's young people can truly understand the anxiety these back-to-back assassinations caused in the United States. It seemed as if our country was unraveling at the seams. The funeral procession for Kennedy passed through the tent city built for the Poor People's Campaign on the Mall in Washington, D.C.

With Kennedy's death, Mama threw herself into working to elect the Humphrey-Muskie presidential ticket. She did not like the Republican candidate, Richard Nixon, one bit, and wanted to make sure a Democrat followed LBJ into the White House. At the end of August, the Democratic Convention in Chicago erupted in rioting and violence over the war in Vietnam. Mama was against the war, and was horrified by the images of police beating protesters.

As a politician, she feared that the chaos of the convention would hurt Democrats at the polls in November. That October, Mama helped organize a Humphrey rally at Norfolk's New Calvary Baptist Church, an event sponsored by the Women for Humphrey Committee, which was headed by her Third Force colleague Vivian Carter Mason. Mama was one of the speakers, and encouraged everyone to participate in a door-to-door, get-out-the-vote campaign for the Democratic candidate. She also served as the director of operations at the local Humphrey office, which operated a phone bank twelve hours a day through the campaign's last week, staffed by housewives and students.

Her fears about the Chicago riots proved to be well-founded. Nixon, promising to restore law and order, won 301 electoral votes, including the state of California. Humphrey trailed with 191, and George Wallace carried five Southern states and forty-six electoral votes. Those results obscured a much closer popular vote—Nixon won 43.4 percent, and Humphrey, 42.7. The Democrat lost Virginia, but carried the state's Second Congressional District, which included Norfolk. It was the only one of Virginia's ten districts that Humphrey won.

In the same election, Virginians repudiated the Byrd Machine's "pay-as-you-go" aversion to debt by passing an $81 million bond issue to finance new mental health facilities. My mother was among twenty-six people appointed to a steering committee that campaigned heavily in support of the bond issue.

Though Byrd's Massive Resistance gambit had been defeated in 1958, equal education for black children was still not a reality ten years later. Booker T. Washington High School had long been the only black high school in the city. After the walkout and the protests of 1963, the School Board announced plans to abandon the building entirely, and to build a new one on Tidewater Drive about six miles north of its existing location.

The proposed location was in a lower-income white community. While this might have fostered the integration of black and white students, no black children would be able to walk to the new school.

Most of the black community wanted a new building, but not a new location. In July 1969, Mama served on a steering committee of citizens who called themselves the United Black Federation. The group's sole purpose was to "unify" the black community around convincing the Norfolk School Board to re-build Booker T. Washington in the same spot. The federation launched a petition drive which ultimately collected 10,400 sig-natures in support of the goal.

Members of the steering committee who attended the initial meeting and unanimously agreed to keep Booker T. in Norfolk's Brambleton neighborhood included some of the black commu-nity's established and emerging leaders—my mother, Father Joseph N. Green Jr., the pastor of Grace Episcopal Church; Lenious G. Bond and Rev. Ben A Beamer Sr.; Dr. William P Robinson, Sr., Mr. Jordan's one-time rival, and his son, William P. Robinson Jr., better known as Billy; Frank Bowe, Dr. Milton A. Reid, and Williams Giddens; Bishop D. Lawrence Williams, Calvin M. Jacox, and George Banks; James Gay; and not least, a tall, baritone-voiced minister and budding radio personality, Rev. Levi E. Willis.

Their effort demonstrated the veracity of the first lesson of my mother's life. It is not enough to express political opinions. You must work with like-minded individuals on specific goals and use the law, when necessary, to accomplish them. The drive to keep Booker T. where it was led to a lawsuit, which Judge Hoffman decided in 1971. The school stayed put.

Finally, in 1969, newly registered black voters helped bring about the demise of the Byrd Machine that had dominated Virginia politics since 1929. That year, neither of the Byrd candidates for governor or lieutenant governor made it through the Democratic primary. In a *Journal and Guide* column called "Watch on the Potomac," Robert Spivack observed that the rest of the country was moving to the right, while staid old Virginia was veering slightly to the left. Why? Because, he wrote, the Byrd Machine had been in power too long.

That fall, Virginia voters elected a Republican governor, A. Linwood Holton, ending eighty-four years of Southern Democratic rule. William P. Robinson Sr. won a seat in the House of Delegates, becoming the first black to do so since Reconstruction.

My mother received her first appointment to a citywide biracial organization in 1969. The Urban Coalition was Norfolk's effort to coordinate all private and public programs related to problems of the poor, and to ensure that these various programs were truly responsive to the city's needs. Funds for the program came from the business community, labor, religious groups, and civic organizations. Initially, the chair was white, but within a few years, my mother's friend, the courtly Father Joe Green, was elected to head the organization.

One of my favorite photos of Mama comes from this period. In 1970, The Women of Virginia's Third Force took its annual trip to Richmond to meet with elected officials. They wanted to show support for a piece of legislation by Senator Babalas that called for the formation of a state human rights commission. In a group photo of eleven black women, three black men and three white men, my mother is standing left of center next to Lieutenant Governor J. Sargeant Reynolds, heir to his family's aluminum fortune. She is smiling broadly and he is shaking her hand, but it looks as if they're holding hands. The *Journal and Guide* pointed that out, commenting: "Nothing wrong with that, is there?"

In 1970, four years after Mama's Supreme Court victory, the General Assembly passed a "use it or lose it" law that purged voters from the registration rolls if they had not voted at least once in the previous four years. Someone who showed up at the polls on Election Day might find that he or she had lost the right to vote in that election, and would have to re-register for the next one. In Virginia, it was always something.

Because of her experience helping to save Oakwood from demolition and redevelopment, my mother became intensely interested in the future of housing in Norfolk. She got involved in the Model Cities program, which the U.S. Department of Housing and Urban Development had created as part of Lyndon Johnson's War on Poverty. The program had a short life span, ending in 1974, after just eight years. But it had ambitious aims, among them to involve citizens in the renewal of blighted urban neighborhoods and industrial lands, and to boost the quality of life for residents of those areas—in health, education, employment, transportation, and safety from crime. Model Cities sought to build stronger communities, not just buildings. The Norfolk Model Cities program focused on the neighborhoods of Berkley, Brambleton, Huntersville, East Ghent and Ghent, all areas encircling the city's central business district and on both sides of the Elizabeth River. Residents from other neighborhoods were expected to participate, so that the entire city could claim authorship of the program. In 1972, Mama was elected by her peers to serve as a member of the Model Cities Commission, and a year later she was given an award for her outstanding service to the program and the city's residents.

This recognition was followed in 1974 by her appointment to the bi-racial Citizens Advisory Committee. Mama's good friend Alice Green was one of the early appointees to the CAC, soon after it was established in 1962—but she was not reappointed in 1965. Mrs. Green lambasted the CAC a "do-nothing" group in public. "To those of you who are not aware or who do not recall, it should be interesting to note that the CAC was formed to prevent the federal government from cutting off the millions of dollars received by the City of Norfolk through the Norfolk Redevelopment and Housing Authority," she said. She continued:

The rules under which federal money and credits are granted require that there be a representative local committee named, which is kept informed of, and which may give advice on, urban renewal planning. No such committee existed in Norfolk. That is, no such committee existed until the Oakwood-Rosemont Civic League engaged counsel, and complained to the Housing and Home Finance Agency. Mayor Duckworth eventually named a Citizens Advisory Committee in January of 1962. Although there are many, many problems connected with urban renewal, the CAC was a do-nothing committee, which did nothing very well—by subcommittee. During July of 1963, following many requests to City Council for a human relations committee to serve the problems of race relations, the Citizens Advisory Committee was given the additional duty of handling racial matters. Now we have two duties: urban renewal and race problems. Either duty, if performed well, could more than utilize the full time of CAC. But since we were doing nothing on urban renewal, we certainly had time to do nothing on racial matters, and we did just that. No doubt the best service I can render to my fellow citizens is to point out that the CAC is only so much window dressing which will never become more until indignant citizens require more of it. Thanks to (chairman) Mr. Ripley and Mayor Martin, I am now relieved of the crushing burden of dual idleness.

As I mentioned, Alice Green and her husband had moved to Virginia Beach when Rosemont was torn down and redeveloped. The CAC may have evolved by the time my mother was appointed to it, because I don't remember her criticizing it the way Mrs. Green did in 1965.

By that time, I was watching my mother's political evolution from afar. I was living in California's Bay Area with my two children, Jimmie and Evelyn, after separating from my first husband. Both of my sisters had moved there in the 1960s, and I lived first with my sister Patricia and her husband, Steve, and their children Tonya and Gus. After a short time in San Diego, we moved back to the Bay Area and stayed with my sister Jeanette, her husband, Jimmie, and their daughter, Cheryl. Perhaps having all her children and grandchildren on the West Coast gave our mother the freedom to pursue her political career with more focus. I know she missed us because we talked on the phone often, especially after the long-distance rates went down at 11 p.m.

The year 1974 was unique in the history of American democracy. A president who had been elected in a forty-nine-state landslide resigned rather than face impeachment. White Norfolk had joined the landslide for Nixon in 1972, but the black community had voted solidly against him. In Mama's precinct, Rosemont, the vote was 1,489 for the Democratic candidate, George McGovern, and just 97 for Nixon. Campostella, a black neighborhood south of the river, voted 1,050 for McGovern to 127 for Nixon. Young Park, the city's biggest public housing project, gave McGovern 1,640 votes and Nixon, 128.

This bloc voting was reflected in local races as well, and it brought citywide attention to the Goldenrod ballot. Black journalist Marvin Lake wrote an in-depth analysis piece for *The Virginian-Pilot*. The piece explored whether rumors that candidates paid for a spot on the Goldenrod were true. Mayor Martin called the Concerned Citizens' endorsement process political bossism. Was he right?

One failed candidate told Lake that without the Goldenrod, "you're dead. Especially in a close race." A black precinct committeeman said, "I've seen the time when the Goldenrod ballot didn't mean anything downtown; now they respect it." Accusations of payment were refuted by several candidates who found themselves listed without seeking the group's endorsement. Candidates for the ballot were selected by a nominating committee, with input from committeemen in the city's twelve black precincts. Any donations to the Concerned Citizens were used to pay for election guide ballots and to supply transportation and lunches to poll workers.

There was nothing illegal in the process, and no pockets lined, but questions about the Concerned Citizens and the Goldenrod lingered—and not surprisingly, because an endorsement on the ballot was a powerful tool and the group was beyond the control of the city's white leadership. That remained the case, and Mama's strong personality was one of the organization's chief protections. She had made a name for herself fighting the establishment in the poll tax case. As chair of Concerned Citizens, she used that reputation and her resulting political clout to get out the vote for candidates who stood for justice.

In the summer of 1975, Mama traded her position on the CAC to become the first black woman appointed a commissioner of the Norfolk Redevelopment and Housing Authority. It was an unpaid position, but extremely prestigious. Mr. Jordan, who was now the city's vice mayor—a post to which he was elected by his fellow members of the Norfolk City Council—nominated her. Not surprisingly, the council's vote was split.

That fall, she went to a nationwide housing authority conference in Los Angeles. Afterwards she flew up to Northern California to visit us. I told her that I had signed up to join the Air Force. Though she was a liberal and a feminist, she thought that was a strange thing for a single mother to do. There were very few women in the service in the mid-1970s. Perhaps she feared that America would become engaged in another Vietnam conflict. I was surprised at how tradition-bound her reaction was. She did not want me to join the service.

That November, Mama was the subject of a *The Virginian-Pilot* article headlined, "New member takes NRHA to task on Berkley housing." She accused the agency of "foot-dragging" on building low and moderate-income housing. She also criticized it for refusing to work with a minority-owned construction firm. Several commissioners and the executive director said they doubted the firm could secure financing to complete a town-house project, based on its record building homes for the Model Cities program, which by this time had been dismantled by the federal government.

In March 1976, she again clashed with her fellow commissioners, this time over a housing authority Affirmative Action plan that she believed to be overly vague. She suggested the plan spell out exactly how blacks would be moved from low-level, low-paying jobs into managerial positions. One male commissioner was particularly dismissive of her input. The newspaper referred to their exchange as the "Alfred and Evelyn Show." She was the lone vote against the Affirmative Action plan.

Those defeats notwithstanding, in the twelve years she served as commissioner, Mama gradually turned her critics into supporters and succeeded in advocating for minority-owned businesses. She repeatedly questioned why millions of federal dollars "designed to help make life better for Norfolk's poor" had been spent on administrative costs, while poor people were being forced out of their homes. By late 1976, the minority-owned construction firm she'd backed, Norfolk Housing Development Corporation, was approved to build a dozen single-family homes, which would be financed by the minority-owned Atlantic National Bank.

Reflecting on her early years as a commissioner, she told Marvin Lake, "When I first went on the housing authority, I felt that there was no one there that really was interested in what happened to poor people" who were displaced by redevelopment. "I felt somebody needed to be there to see that those people received help.

"And with each project that was taking place with NRHA, I would always get calls from poor people who could not afford to move or felt like they had not gotten their right share of relocation money. And these things I would report to the executive director, and he would check into it and make sure that they got their fair share of relocation and were moved into a place where they could afford to pay rent or maybe buy."

This is the third lesson to take from my mother's life: Be true to your principles. Know your constituents' needs and fight for them. And don't give up when people in power say "no" the first time you bring up an issue.

According to an NRHA report, over the six years beginning in January 1974, an estimated $106 million was invested in Norfolk's redevelopment program. Over 1,700 housing units were constructed, while 618 residences and 128 commercial structures were demolished. The authority rehabilitated 536 substandard housing units. Downtown office space grew by more than a half-million square feet, and hotel rooms by five hundred. The authority relocated 1,800 households and 225 businesses.

Among Mama's most pressing concerns was adequate housing for seniors. She supported the construction of Braywood Manor in Rosemont, a nine-story high-rise that provided 228 low-income units. It was approved in 1977, and opened in 1980.

She also supported the redevelopment of the downtown waterfront. "When I first came into the redevelopment authority, I would go around the country on different conventions and I would come back to Norfolk and I felt shame," she told the *Pilot*'s Marvin Lake. Along the Elizabeth River shoreline, "there were broken piers all the way up to the coal terminal"—a mile downriver—"and it looked bad from our side of Norfolk. I felt that we should do something about that.

In other words, her focus expanded beyond her own community. "You have to be interested in the city as a whole—to be able to say that you've got to do something downtown and you've got to do something uptown, too," she explained. "There's a need for more public housing, there's a need for more affordable housing, and there's a need for the housing that we did downtown in those old warehouses to bring our tax dollars into the city."

"It was an overall thing I was looking at," she said. "If you go downtown now and look at Norfolk and all those buildings that we're getting built there, you feel proud of it."

Here is a fourth lesson that she learned quickly in her time as a housing commissioner: Be supportive of others' goals. She advocated not only for the poor, but recognized the needs of the business community and those of the city as a whole.

She still criticized the authority when she felt it was necessary, however. In 1977, she and the other black housing commissioner, Franklin Thornton, protested the selection of David Rice, a white man, as NRHA's new executive director. My mother questioned "how an all-white planning department can determine what is good for the well-being of the majority of blacks in Norfolk who are directly affected by the housing authority." Mr. Thornton argued that Affirmative Action "should start at the top." Both were critical of the apparent secrecy involved in the selection process. "It was in the local papers that Rice had been chosen for the job before the commission even had a chance to vote on the matter," Mama complained. Nevertheless, she promised to "wait and see" how the new administration would work with the black community.

CHAPTER TEN

HARD LESSONS

Mama continued to be active in Democratic politics on the local and national level. She helped re-elect Joe Jordan to City Council in 1972 and 1976, and was on the steering committee for the reelection of William Robinson to the House of Delegates in 1971. She worked on Jimmy Carter's presidential campaign in 1976, and had the opportunity to meet Rosalynn Carter when she came to Norfolk a month before the election. The Carters had lived in the Norfolk area when the future president was in the navy and their first son was born there. Virginia was the only southern state that did not award its electoral votes to Carter, but he did receive more votes than the Republican incumbent, Gerald Ford, in Norfolk, Portsmouth, and Chesapeake.

She also campaigned for Chuck Robb when he entered politics by running for lieutenant governor of Virginia in 1977. Robb had entered the public eye when, as a Marine assigned to the Corps' presidential detail, he'd romanced Lynda Bird

Johnson, LBJ's older daughter. The couple had married in the White House in 1967. When Robb campaigned in Norfolk, he held a press conference at Mama's house, because they wanted the community to know she supported his candidacy. He even stayed at her house instead of a hotel.

My cousin Roxanne, Rosanna's daughter, was a teenager at the time, and performed chores for Mama in exchange for alterations or sewing. She cleaned the house for his visit, and teased Mama about it: "He don't have enough money to stay at a hotel? Dude must be hard up the best he can do is stay in Oakwood." Mama shushed her, explaining, "It's politics." When he came out of the bedroom wearing a bathrobe to take a shower, Roxanne worried that he had overheard her. When Robb recalled the visit in 2017, he said he always stayed at his friends' homes when he campaigned. He had one clear memory of his stay with Mama: "She sent me off with a good breakfast."

That was the same year that Mr. Jordan was appointed a judge in Norfolk's General District Court. After taking his place on the bench he was no longer active in politics, but he and Mama remained good friends.

By 1978, my father's disability had become noticeably worse. He was seventy-one years old and confined to a wheelchair. I was married again, in the Air Force, and had orders to go to Germany. My mother's feelings about my military career had evolved. She saw what a great opportunity it was proving to be, and she adored my new husband, Staff Sergeant Robert Ligon.

The only negative experience I'd had in my first years in the service occurred in Minot, North Dakota, where a landlord refused to rent an apartment to me because I was black. He told me it was rented, but told a white colleague that it was available. The base housing office contacted the Department of Housing and Urban Development, which sent a representative from Denver. She couldn't work out anything with the landlord. Being my mother's daughter, I called the ACLU in Denver, which filed a lawsuit on my behalf. It was in the newspaper and on television. The landlord did business on base and he was mortified by the coverage. He wanted the issue to go away, so we settled out of court. By that time, I had found an apartment elsewhere.

My son and daughter had lived with my parents for six months in 1976, while I was in basic training and technical school. When we visited them two years later on our way to Germany, they were making plans to move out of the little shotgun house on Kennedy Street where they had lived for thirty years. Due to his 100-percent military disability, Daddy was eligible for a Veterans Administration grant to renovate the house to make it accessible for his wheelchair. An architect Mama hired told her it wasn't feasible—the doors could not be widened, and the front yard wasn't deep enough for a ramp from the front door to the sidewalk. So, they applied the VA allowance for renovating the house to the construction of a new wheelchair-accessible home in nearby Rosemont. Their new neighborhood was a subdivision called Meadowbrook Woods that was part of Rosemont's redevelopment. The VA grant and the sale of the old house made the new place comfortably affordable.

On Election Day in November 1979, *The Virginian-Pilot* published a feature about my mother, illustrated with a photo depicting her at the Forty-second Precinct's polling place. The image captured her clutching a computer printout of voters' names as she shouted instructions to one of her workers. The article paid tribute to her ability to deliver black votes to Democrats and her skill as an organizer. She did her homework to get out the vote. She arrived at the poll at 6 a.m. sharp, bringing a lunch with her. The computer printout was color-coded, and marked an improvement over the handwritten lists of the past. After a person cast a vote, she checked off his or her name on the printout. She knew everyone in the neighborhood, and often dispatched drivers to the homes of people who had not yet voted. She kept four cars and drivers on hand for this service. The story described how postal workers, arriving at the polls at 6 a.m., were turned away because the voting machines weren't working—and how Mama knew the names of all of them, and made sure they voted after work. Republicans did not even bother to show up in her precinct. "They know better," Mama told the reporter. "Wouldn't do them any good."

The next day, an election analysis by *Pilot* reporter Marvin Lake and his colleague Don Hunt described the situation plainly. The black vote determined the winner, and blacks did not vote Republican. One frustrated G.O.P. member said that the Ayatollah Ruhollah Khomeini could win Norfolk's black vote if his name was on the Goldenrod ballot.

Sadly, my father passed away the next day—November 9, 1979. He became ill with pneumonia and never recovered. It was a shock for my mother. She was fifty-five years old and already a widow. My family flew home from Germany. My baby Robin had been born in Germany, and we had to get her traveling documents on short notice. It was not long after the hostages had been taken in Iran, and the American Embassy was surrounded by German police, but to make a long and nerve-wracking story short, we made it to the United States for the funeral, and Daddy was buried on my birthday, November 14. My sisters and their children had flown in from California.

When we all left for home, I worried about Mama. She had been surrounded by family and extended family all her life. For the first time, she would be living alone. But my aunts Pudney, Bunky, and Rosanna were still in Norfolk, and they rallied around her. The Women of Virginia's Third Force had been planning to honor her at a banquet, and now the event took on a special significance. The announcement read, "All too often, we fall into a system where the normal outstanding day-to-day contributions tend to be taken for granted, so we pause to acknowledge the many noteworthy contributions made by Mrs. Butts in the interest of mankind." One of the highlights of the evening was a presentation—"This is Your Life, Politically."

The presentation must have lifted her spirits and boosted her confidence, because a few months later, she decided to run for Norfolk City Council. She had never considered running for office herself, because she was more comfortable working behind the scenes, helping other candidates and organizing support for causes. But her friends put the idea in her head: They told her she was at the height of her popularity, and it was time for a black woman to break into politics in Norfolk.

My mother had never earned a dime for the political work she'd done to that point. City Council members were paid a small salary. Now that Daddy had passed away, she was receiving a widow's pension. Working for a salary would take away the stress of trying to make ends meet while paying the mortgage on the new house. She threw her hat in the ring.

When she announced her candidacy in February 1980, *The Virginian-Pilot* ran an article that characterized my mother as a black candidate who could not win support in the white community. That canard would stick to her every time she ran for office. It was an unfair description, given her work with the NRHA and her support for downtown development and renewal of the waterfront. A tax-revolt organization calling itself the Norfolk Tea Party opposed her candidacy, citing her unwillingness to cut taxes—she believed it would reduce funding to the city's schools. The *Pilot* story predicted that her name would appear on the Goldenrod ballot, because she was a prominent member of Concerned Citizens.

A few days before the election, another *Pilot* article announced that both my mother and a white candidate—Betty Howell, wife of Virginia's former lieutenant governor, Henry Howell—would be endorsed on the Goldenrod. Thousands of flyers would be distributed in the black community, ensuring thousands of votes for both candidates. Still, it was a risky move for Concerned Citizens to put both candidates on the Goldenrod. "Although Mrs. Howell received its endorsement in her 1974 and 1978 council campaigns, some of the group's members had suggested that Mrs. Howell's appearance on the guide ballot this year could give her enough black votes to hurt Mrs. Butts' chances of victory in a close election," the newspaper reported.

The conservative strategy would have been to "single shot" my mother, to ensure that she alone would receive the bulk of the black community's support. But the Howells were leaders of the so-called populist wing of the Democratic Party, and Concerned Citizens had a longstanding relationship with them.

On Election Day, Betty Howell was the top vote-getter, thanks to support from both the white establishment and the black community. Mama came in fourth in a race for three open council seats. She performed well overall—there were twelve candidates, and she trounced eight of them. But she fell 414 votes short of success. A few days later, *The Virginian-Pilot* published a story headlined "Mrs. Butts Attacks Howell Staff," and accompanied by an unflattering picture of Mama with her mouth open, looking very angry. The two campaigns had agreed to help each other. Mrs. Howell was supposed to have precinct workers distribute the Goldenrod ballot in the white community to boost votes for my mother. A supporter called from a white precinct, Crossroads Elementary, and reported, "Mrs. Butts, there's nothing here with your name on it."

With the benefit of hindsight, I think there might be a fifth lesson to draw from my mother's political life: In the words of Kenny Rogers, "know when to hold them, and know when to fold them." The next nine years in my mother's political career were filled with disappointments and betrayals. I wish she'd had a crystal ball and could have avoided them.

A few weeks after the election, I came home from Germany with the baby for Mama's birthday. It was a surprise, and she was thrilled to see us. We went to Virginia Beach for dinner with Bunky. Mama was in fine spirits. Though she regretted the loss, she had no burning desire to run again. Some people recommended transitioning from at-large citywide elections to a ward system to ensure that more black candidates could be elected. Mama was not convinced it was a good idea, but she kept an open mind about the issue.

She was focusing her energies on applying to take care of disabled veterans in need of housing. Now that she had a three-bedroom home outfitted for the disabled, she figured she might put it to good use and supplement her income with rent money.

It was a presidential election year, so Mama volunteered for Jimmy Carter's re-election campaign. She was a delegate to the city and state Democratic conventions, and was elected to be a delegate for Carter at the national convention in New York City in August. I don't think she had been to the city since her family's residency in the 1930s. I imagine she was both excited and nervous to make the trip. I was still stationed in Germany, and did not have a phone. I received a message from my supervisor that my sister Jeanette had called: My mother was in intensive care in a New York hospital. She'd had surgery for an intestinal hernia when I was in sixth or seventh grade, and the condition returned with a vengeance during the convention. I know that Senator Babalas tried to visit her at the hospital, but was not allowed to see her. Jeanette flew to New York from California and stayed with her until she was ready to fly home.

After she recuperated, Mama went back to campaigning. Rosalynn Carter came to Norfolk to make a speech and my mother sat next to her on the stage.

I cannot begin to describe her disappointment at Ronald Reagan's election. She was deeply offended when he made a speech in Neshoba County, Mississippi, after the Republican convention, in which he praised "states' rights." What message could he possibly be sending about states' rights—a code phrase if ever there was one—in the very place where three civil rights workers had been kidnapped and slain in 1964? Mama also dreaded what Reagan had in mind for housing programs for the poor. She worried about the continual decline in federal housing dollars.

By the end of the year, the first disabled elderly veterans moved into her house. Two or three of them lived with her for the next thirteen years. One, Joe, lived with her until she died. She was required to feed them, which she did a little bit too well—she made full meals for breakfast, lunch and dinner. The social workers noted that the men were putting on weight, so they told her that perhaps a sandwich for lunch would be enough.

January 1981 brought sad news for the black community. William P. Robinson Sr., the first black elected to the House of Delegates in the twentieth century, died of bone cancer. His death represented a fault line between the black politics of old in Norfolk, and the politics to come—the former, my mother's generation of civil rights leaders, was giving way to a rising generation. For Mama, the transition would prove to be brutal.

Dr. Robinson's obituary in the *Journal and Guide* paid tribute to his incredible physical strength. In the last four years of his life, he served in the legislature and taught classes at Norfolk State in excruciating pain. The respect of his colleagues earned him the chairmanship of the Health, Welfare and Institutions Committee. He served on a subcommittee studying the allocation of highway maintenance funding and manpower, presided over the Conference of Black Elected Officials in Virginia, and was on the steering committee for Concerned Citizens. Those who knew him well described him as an educated, eloquent man who was respectful of people from all backgrounds. "He could put himself in another person's shoes," my mother told the paper. "He was a kind and warm person that understood the needs of others. Norfolk has lost a great citizen that worked up to his last day to try to improve conditions." A month after his death, his son, William P. Robinson, Jr., a Harvard-educated lawyer, won a special election to take his father's seat in the legislature. He won the seat again in the regular election that November.

Mama decided to start a new political tradition: An early-morning breakfast meeting at her house each month for members of Concerned Citizens, prepared and served up by the Women of Virginia's Third Force. The regulars were Marie Young, my mother's friend from the picket lines and the Third Force; Rev. Joe Green, who'd taken Joe Jordan's seat on the City Council when Mr. Jordan became a judge; and Yvonne Miller, head of the Department of Education at Norfolk State University. Dr. Miller had ambitions to run for House of Delegates, and Mama was a mentor to her. Others at the breakfasts included James Rivers, the secretary of Concerned Citizens; Delegate "Billy" Robinson; a successful businessman named Tom Graves; and Bishop Levi E. Willis, the minister and businessman.

While Mr. Jordan and Billy Robinson were politically prominent, many Norfolkians considered Bishop Willis to wield even more influence in the black community, in part because he was successful and wealthy. He owned a network of radio stations scattered around the country, which he oversaw from a headquarters in Norfolk. He had founded the Garden of Prayer, a church with a large congregation.

He was often described as a self-made man. He and his six siblings had grown up in a one-room sharecropper's shack in North Carolina, and he once recalled that their poverty was so dire they did not know whether they'd survive. The family moved to Norfolk in 1945, when Willis was sixteen. After some years in Philadelphia—where he was shot in a street fight—he returned to Norfolk and began his long climb to a better life. He was ordained in the Church of God in Christ, started a one-room church, and in 1970 became the youngest chairman elected to COGIC's national bishops' council. He was a gifted charismatic preacher. He bought rental properties and soon owned one hundred of them, which he sold when he got into radio. He was South Hampton Roads's first black radio operator, and methodically added small stations to his portfolio until he owned twenty-three, generating millions of dollars in revenue. He also hosted a call-in program titled "Crusade for Christ" that aired on his stations.

He became board chairman and a majority stockholder of Atlantic National Bank, the first bank in the area with biracial ownership. He also owned funeral homes, and thus had forged personal relationships with many black Norfolk families. When he ate with the Concerned Citizens at my mother's table, he was rich and important—but was hungry for more than breakfast. "The bishop," as he was known, was not yet politically powerful. That's why he was there: He wanted to be head of Concerned Citizens. As he ate Mama's biscuits, eggs and bacon, he was mulling how he might convince her to step aside, to leave the organization she'd midwifed into existence and prominence. She had no clue what was coming.

My mother advocated for two causes close to her heart in 1981. One was the election of Chuck Robb as Virginia's governor. That October she appeared on the front page of the *Journal and Guide* while speaking at a campaign rally organized by the Women of Virginia's Third Force. Around her were Robb's wife, Lynda, and her mother, Lady Bird Johnson, the former first lady and widow of President Lyndon Johnson. Robb won with a comfortable 53.3 percent of the vote.

The other was the commercial redevelopment of Norfolk's waterfront, a project called "Waterside," and it was not nearly so easy a sell. Vocal critics questioned whether the taxpayers should risk $13 million on a marketplace-style mall of restaurants and shops on the Elizabeth River waterfront. Mama supported the project officially as an NRHA commissioner. It was one of her proudest accomplishments. She told the *Pilot*'s Marvin Lake, "I felt this was something that would help the city's tax base and bring tax money into the city."

Meanwhile, Mama had changed her mind about never running for office again. In mid-January 1982, she announced her candidacy for Norfolk City Council. She'd lost by such a narrow margin the first time around, and thought now that if she announced earlier, and ran on a ticket with Joe Green, rather than a white candidate, it would assure her a seat on the panel.

It was to prove a contentious election, however. Nine days after she announced her candidacy, a committee of the Norfolk School Board announced plans to eliminate busing for elementary schools. Busing had never been popular in the white community, and the issue was much in the news during the campaign season. By the 1980s, Norfolk was busing 29,000 students through 1.7 million miles of the city's streets every year, and spending $4 million to do it. When busing had started in 1970, Norfolk's school enrollment was 56,830 students, of which 57 percent were white and 43 percent were black. By ten years later, enrollment had dropped to 35,540, and the percentages had flipped—black students accounted for 58 percent of the district's total enrollment, and white students, 42 percent. Furthermore, Norfolk's population had declined by 13 percent during the 1970s, while Virginia Beach's increased by 50 percent and Chesapeake's by 28 percent. Reagan's Justice Department opposed mandatory busing. The Norfolk School Board, white parents, and the business community were all in agreement that busing had served its purpose, and now needed to end for the sake of the city's financial health and the school district's continued viability.

Some parents in the black community agreed. Many did not, including my mother. Undoubtedly, her support for busing cost her votes from the white community. And she was not the only candidate vying for votes in the black community: Two activists, James Gay, now an attorney, and Herbert Collins, a grocery store owner, also entered the race—and both claimed that Concerned Citizens had lost touch with the black community. It came as a shock when the city's Democratic Party endorsed four candidates for council—two whites and two blacks—who were also Democratic Committee members, and none of whom were my mother. This was a slap in the face after all the work she'd done on behalf of the party to steer black votes to white Democratic candidates.

Concerned Citizens had endorsed the former state party chair, Joe Fitzpatrick, in his race for city treasurer in 1981, and he won my mother's precinct by the overwhelming margin of 1,483 to 21. In the wake of the party endorsements, *The Virginian-Pilot* published an article reporting that some members of Concerned Citizens feared that now Fitzpatrick was out to split the black vote to start his own political machine. His supporters said he was recovering from back surgery when the endorsements were made, and that the decision was the work of an ad-hoc committee. Still, the wisdom of making the endorsements was questioned by many in the article.

On Election Day, the Democratic Party compounded the insult by distributing a sample ballot on yellow paper, imitating the Goldenrod ballot, which confused voters. It contained the pictures of Gay, Collins, city party chair William Williams, and committee member Carolyn Papafil. Joe Green was easily reelected, but Mama trailed the winners by 3,250 votes. The three winning white candidates were opposed to busing.

She earned about 10,000 more votes than the four candidates endorsed by the Democratic Party, however, sending a clear message. "You cannot come in our community and run our affairs," Reverend Green told the newspaper: "We run our own affairs." If Collins and Gay had stayed out of the race, my mother surely would have been elected the second black on the council. She announced that she would definitely run again.

CHAPTER ELEVEN

A RUINOUS RIVALRY

While Mama planned a third run for the council, much was happening around her. Herbert Collins and James Gay believed their 1982 loss—which was far more pronounced than Mama's— could be blamed on Norfolk's system of at-large voting. They became plaintiffs in an NAACP lawsuit, *Collins v. City of Norfolk*, seeking to replace at-large voting with a system of wards. If the city were carved into pieces, each electing one member of the council, the seven-member panel was surely going to have two black members, they believed, and probably three or four. The lawsuit began a slow, meandering journey through the federal court system.

That summer, Governor Robb appointed Mama to the state Board of Housing and Community Development. The board was responsible for apportioning community development funds to smaller municipalities. She was greatly honored by the appointment and traveled to Richmond throughout the year for meetings.

She enjoyed successes on the NRHA board, too. After eight years on the panel, Mama found she did not have to push as hard to influence her colleagues. In March 1983, for example, she voted against assisting a corporation set up to administer loans from the Small Business Administration. The newly formed corporation had no one on its board from Church Street and Huntersville, two black neighborhoods undergoing redevelopment. Mama didn't see the sense in that, and said so—and none of her fellow commissioners seconded a motion by the chair to provide office space to the group. The company's vice president promised to appoint someone from Church Street and Huntersville.

My mother had victories playing to her strengths as an organizer, as well. She had the great pleasure of supporting Yvonne Miller in her campaign to be the first black woman to run for House of Delegates. Like Chuck Robb, Ms. Miller announced her candidacy in April 1983 from my mother's house. Mama at that time was Chairman of the Second Congressional District for the Democratic Party, as well as chairperson of Concerned Citizens. Ms. Miller was an academic at Norfolk State, but had limited political experience. She considered Mama "the master" of Norfolk politics, and Mama adopted her as a protégé. She was so proud when her friend became Delegate Miller, and later still, Senator Miller.

But 1983 was, in the main, apocalyptic for my mother, and for Norfolk. The literal translation of the Greek word apocalypse is "that which is hidden will be revealed." So it was: Bishop Willis made a decisive foray into politics when he invited the Reverend Jesse Jackson to Norfolk in May to lead a march in support of busing. That spring, the Norfolk School Board had filed a pleading in U.S. District Court seeking approval of its plan for eliminating elementary school busing. It also filed suit against four black parents, and some of their children, who were opposed to the plan. Forcing parents to bear the financial burden of defending a lawsuit was unheard of. Bishop Willis and one of the defendants, King Davis, formed an ad hoc Committee of Concerned Citizens in response to the controversial strategy.

In April, the board dropped the suit, bowing to community outrage. Several parents who were opposed to ending busing filed a lawsuit on behalf of their children, alleging in *Riddick v. School Board of the City of Norfolk* that a return to neighborhood schools illegally discriminated against black students. Norfolk's segregated housing patterns assured that a return to neighborhood schools would be synonymous with a return to segregated schools. A pro-busing march was scheduled for May 13.

Norfolk Mayor Vincent Thomas was worried about the negative national attention that would be drawn by the event. He did not want a repeat of the public relations disaster of Massive Resistance. Late on the night before the planned march, Bishop Willis arranged for a meeting between Jesse Jackson and Thomas at the airport. They held a press conference at 1 a.m., calling for better communication between the black and white communities.

My mother was at the airport meeting. She was also at a breakfast meeting of 225 civil rights activists the next morning. She confided to me and my sisters that Rev. Jackson told her, in effect, that it was time for the women to move over and let the men take the lead. He did not specifically mention Bishop Willis by name, but in years to come, it would become apparent that that was whom he meant. My mother was deeply insulted that Rev. Jackson failed to recognize her contribution to the city and the nation. She contrasted his behavior and attitude with the way Martin Luther King had greeted her almost twenty years before.

Later in the day, Jackson marched at the head of a procession 6,000 strong through the streets to Norfolk City Hall, then delivered a speech that downplayed school desegregation and busing. Instead, he emphasized the need for blacks to gain political power, especially in the statehouse, and he urged people to register to vote.

The unusually large march was significant for several reasons. It showed that thousands of people in Norfolk supported busing and were willing to spend a day protesting for it. It also revealed the deep distrust that the citizens had for their elected leaders. As Ed Brown, president of Local 128 of the International Longshoreman's Association, observed: "The issue is not busing. The issue is the perpetuation of political power by those who are in power at this date."

Paul Riddick, plaintiff in the school busing case, saw the march differently. "This was when the deals started being made in the back rooms," he said. "So the route was changed, and the route ended in downtown Norfolk at City Hall. It was diluted and it turned into a voter registration march. Deals began to be made between some of the power brokers on the west side and Bishop Willis, who was the catalyst from the black community."

Pro-busing advocates threatened a second march for June 1 at the grand opening of Waterside, the waterfront retail development that my mother supported so strongly. After a closed-door meeting between Willis, the mayor, the president of the school board and others including my mother, the board voted to postpone implementation of its neighborhood school assignment plan for another year. Willis regarded the end of busing as inevitable. He would later negotiate with the school district to hire a black superintendent and to appoint a black to chair the school board.

Mama worked hard behind the scenes to dissuade Willis from protesting Waterside because, like the business leaders, she feared a protest would give the new marketplace a bad image. She was bursting with pride about Waterside, which she rightly saw as a catalyst to revitalizing Norfolk's down-at-heels downtown. It contained 82,000 square feet of retail space with 122 restaurants, shops and fast food eateries. Over 100,000 people were expected for the grand opening, which included a parade and evening fireworks. The complex provided 1,000 full-time and part-time jobs, and promised to jumpstart redevelopment in the surrounding blocks. It benefitted the entire city. Mama truly believed and often said, "Waterside is for everyone."

After two losses, she was determined to win her third run for Norfolk City Council. She expected to be the only black candidate on the ballot in 1984, having announced her candidacy to Concerned Citizens at the beginning of January. Imagine her surprise when three ministers stopped by her house ten days later to inform her that one of them was running, too. His name was John Foster, and he was the pastor of Shiloh Baptist Church and the vice-chair of the school board. Rev. Foster was also on the steering committee for Concerned Citizens.

She was shocked by the news. Mama called a friend of hers from the white community—Harvey Lindsay, a real estate entrepreneur who'd helped develop Waterside—to find out if there was something going on behind the scenes that she should know about. Sure enough, there was a backstory. A biracial group had been meeting informally with the mayor to discuss racial problems. Rev. Foster was part of this group, as were more of her own colleagues in Concerned Citizens, among them Rev. Ronnie Joyner and Bishop Willis, whom she learned was serving as Foster's campaign manager. The group believed it was in Norfolk's best interest to have a second black on the seven-member council, and John Foster seemed the perfect candidate, because they reckoned he could attract white votes. The mayor had acknowledged that the black community had tried twice to elect my mother, but she'd fared poorly in white precincts. Harvey Lindsay encouraged her to drop out of the race.

Mama did not follow his advice. She told *The Virginian-Pilot* that she was in the race to stay. She had strong support in the black community, and believed her support for downtown development would earn votes from the white community. Rev. Joyner was circumspect when he was asked why the group did not endorse Mama: "It's a very sensitive matter," he said. "You're dealing with an institution when you're dealing with Mrs. Butts." However, the reporter did not tiptoe around her perceived shortcomings and strengths. "Plain-spoken, opinionated and portly, Mrs. Butts never attended college," the story read. "She is a halting public speaker, and some admirers privately question her ability to deal with complex issues such as budget and finance."

On the positive side, the story noted that she "was a plaintiff in a case in which the U.S. Supreme Court struck down Virginia's poll tax in 1966. And she has encouraged thousands of blacks to become registered voters and to support candidates endorsed by Concerned Citizens. In the past six months alone, she estimates, she has registered nearly 2,000 blacks."

This high number was attributable to the city registrar finally conceding that voter registration could take place outside of Norfolk City Hall. Mama had since then routinely set up registration tables at buildings where poor people applied for food stamps or other government aid.

***

Billy Robinson, sensing the tension in Concerned Citizens, called a meeting of the steering committee at his home. Eleven people gathered, including John Foster, Reverend Joyner, Bishop Willis, and Mama. She told them what Lindsay had relayed to her, that Rev. Foster's candidacy had emerged from the mayor's biracial talks. The others in the room roundly denied his claim. The eleven took a voice vote on whether Concerned Citizens should endorse both Foster and Mama. She opposed the idea. But the vote went against her.

Now, behind the scenes Bishop Willis had spent considerable time and energy trying to get my mother to leave the chairmanship of Concerned Citizens, so that he could take the reins. She had refused, and in response the bishop had founded a rival political advocacy group, the Rainbow Coalition—a local offshoot of Jesse Jackson's national political bloc of the same name. The Norfolk Rainbow Coalition printed several guide ballots aimed at building support for Rev. Foster and two white incumbents the group backed, Betty Howell and Joseph Leafe. My mother's name was conspicuously absent from the Rainbow ballots. If she had been endorsed by both Concerned Citizens and the Rainbow, I believe she could have defeated Joe Leafe.

After six of the ten council candidates were featured on Willis's "Crusade for Christ" call-in radio show, Mama met the bishop in his office. He pedaled on his exercise bike while she told him off for not endorsing her on the Rainbow ballot, when the Goldenrod had backed both black candidates. The *Pilot* reported that she told Bishop Willis: "You and your friends have shown your male chauvinism against an old black woman running for office." He patronized her by calling her "sweetie," and reminded her she had run twice and lost. He tried to blame Mama for the Rainbow ballot omission, reminding her that he and Foster had offered her the chance to run as a ticket, but that she'd refused.

When I picture this scene, it makes me angry and sad. Bishop Willis riding that exercise bike in the office of his radio station captures the gulf separating him from my mother. He had wealth and masculinity and access to power, which he was using to sideline a woman who had devoted her entire life to helping those without wealth or access. Their differences were irreconcilable.

Some outsiders faulted my mother for refusing to compromise and form a coalition with the bishop. But in her defense, she was stung by the callous way they'd tried to shove her aside in favor of Rev. Foster, a relative political neophyte, and their secrecy made it impossible for her to trust them. And from my biased perspective, it's clear to me that she was accustomed to dealing with men like Joe Jordan, Len Holt and Ed Dawley. They did not pursue power for its own sake. They fought injustice to bring equality to those who did not know how to fight for themselves.

Some writers tried to compare the split between Mama and Bishop Willis to the 1966 rivalry between Joe Jordan and William Robinson Sr., when they both ran for a seat in the House of Delegates, and both lost. Mr. Robinson had been endorsed by white backers, while Mr. Jordan had ventured into the fray on his own. But whatever similarities the two situations shared, they were different in key respects. Mr. Jordan and Mr. Robinson were educated lawyers who respected each other. Bishop Willis did not view or treat my mother as an equal. And for her, there was no compromising or working with someone who treated her as though she were inferior.

Contrary to the perception that she could not win white votes, Mama had support from prominent whites in the community. Governor Robb sent her a letter wishing her success in the campaign. She also received letters from Lt. Governor Richard J. Davis and Attorney General Gerald Baliles. She held a biracial press conference attended by Laura Naismith, secretary of the commonwealth, former state Senator Evelyn Hailey, Norfolk attorney Robert Nussbaum, state Senator Stanley Walker, former Delegate Robert Washington, NRHA chair Julian Rashkind, and Robert Stern, chairman of the city's Democratic committee. Prominent among her supporters was House Majority Leader Thomas Moss. In her speech, she promised: "I can assure you, if I am elected I will work to serve whites and blacks together."

Her campaign ads and literature stressed her contributions to the city as a whole, in neighborhood preservation, redevelopment, education, voter registration, and elections. Some of the redevelopment and conservation projects she supported over her NRHA tenure were Downtown West, the Cousteau Ocean Science Center, Carney Park, North Titustown, Church Street and Huntersville Two, the World Trade Center, and Park Place. She supported adding Freemason Street to the National Register of Historic Places.

But she could not overcome the overwhelming political tide running against her. On election day, Rev. Foster's supporters stationed a pastor at every precinct, Yvonne Miller later recalled, and they urged arriving voters to cast their ballots for Foster and Betty Howell. "The pastors at the precincts influenced the people to vote for John Foster, rather than for Mrs. Butts," Miller told me. "And that was very hurtful."

The results were decisive. Rev. Foster was in. For the third time, Mama was out. My mother later told *The Virginian-Pilot* that she'd been defeated not by whites, but by the strength of the black church. "I didn't know they were going to do something like that," she said. "Usually black people have a lot of respect for ministers. They will do whatever ministers ask them to do."

As the numbers rolled in that night, she urged her supporters gathered at the Admiralty Motor Hotel to remain determined. "Don't get dismayed," she told them. "Don't get discouraged because I lost an election. There are so many other things we have to do." She sounded much the same theme to a reporter in attendance. "The Concerned Citizens will keep on," she said. They will continue just as strong as ever." Meanwhile, over at

Rev. Foster's victory party, Bishop Willis announced the election results and one of Foster's supporters shouted, "The Goldenrod is dead! The Rainbow is in!"

I was at the Admiralty Motor Hotel that night. I had a ten-day leave and had come home to help with the election. Campaign headquarters was my mother's living and dining rooms. I made phone calls and took people to the polls on election day. It broke my heart to see her lose. She had worked so hard for so long for everybody. The next day at the house, I saw her anger. I know her sense of betrayal must have broken her heart, too. But she never publicly showed her hurt.

Yvonne Miller empathized with Mama's pain over this third rejection. "I worked under her. I learned from her. She taught me lots of things," she told me. "I used to go over there early in the morning and listen and talk to her, and work with her when she was working on elections.

"There were people who were so stupid as to think that because a person had degrees it meant something. It didn't mean a thing. I was never smarter than Mrs. Butts."

There were other disappointments on the way.

In July 1984, the Riddick case was decided in U.S. District Court. Judge John Mackenzie felt the current school board was "trying to meet the threat posed by white flight and to increase the level of parental involvement" by returning to neighborhood schools. He did not detect discriminatory intent in the board's strategy. The judge was also impressed that black school board members and administrators helped design the modified desegregation plan. The plaintiffs appealed.

It was a presidential election year. Jesse Jackson was a candidate for the Democratic nomination, and Bishop Willis was credited with securing his surprise win in Virginia's Democratic primary. Mama did not work for his campaign, and she did not vote for him; she worked hard for the eventual Democratic standard-bearer, Walter Mondale, and his running mate, Geraldine Ferraro. She was again disappointed, but not surprised, by Ronald Reagan's re-election.

Now that two blacks had been elected to the seven-member Norfolk City Council, political observers reckoned that at-large elections might be able to deliver even greater representation for the city's blacks. Because blacks comprised 35 percent of the population, the thinking went, they should be able to garner three seats. The NAACP lawsuit seeking to replace at-large elections with a ward system differed with that view, arguing that whites controlled Norfolk's political process—and indeed, John Foster was anointed, as much as elected, the second black on the council.

But the suit failed in U.S. District Court in 1985. The court found no discrimination based on factors such as responsiveness to the particular needs and interests of minority groups, or the presence of voting practices that enhanced the opportunity for discrimination, such as provisions outlawing single shot ballots. Mama, Judge Jordan and Billy Robinson were all opposed to a ward system, and provided affidavits saying so to the court. Judge Jordan's comments were quoted in *The Virginian-Pilot:* "It provides all citizens, particularly blacks, to have influence on the City Council. I am strongly opposed to segregated elections as I am opposed to segregated economics or segregated social lives. And a ward system is segregation. It's certainly a contradiction on the part of the NAACP after spending millions to desegregate schools and businesses... to seek segregated politics.

You can't have it both ways. We either are an integrated society or we are not." Mama wrote that disputes within the black community were responsible for her 1982 loss, rather than minority vote dilution. Judge Jordan agreed with her. The plaintiffs appealed to the Fourth U.S. Circuit Court of Appeals.

The lawsuit served to highlight the polarized opinions of the black community.

Mama had supported plaintiff James Gay years before, when he was an up-and-coming activist. Now the lawyer dismissed her contributions, and even told people that "all she did was provide lunch."

Virginia's election of November 1985 marked a historic milestone: L. Douglas Wilder was elected the state's first black lieutenant governor. Mama had met Doug Wilder through her work for Chuck Robb, and was an enthusiastic supporter of his candidacy. She admired his backbone in fighting racism. In 1982, while a state senator, he'd announced his intention to run as an independent candidate for the U.S. Senate seat vacated by Harry Byrd Jr. His candidacy was a protest against Owen Pickett, a Democrat who had praised the outgoing senator's father, Harry Byrd Sr.—the architect of Massive Resistance—for his "independence," in his speech announcing his candidacy. Praising Byrd was a dog whistle to whites who understood that Pickett was pushing the racial status quo.

Wilder knew he had no chance of winning. He simply wanted to force Pickett to withdraw his name from the race, and it worked: Both Pickett and Wilder withdrew, and a Republican was elected to the seat. Some thought Wilder had been a disloyal Democrat, but he did not care. The era of Jim Crow was dead, and no black voter in Virginia would allow a politician to praise one of its fiercest advocates.

At the end of 1985, during the Norfolk City Democratic Committee elections, the polarization of Norfolk's black community was again on display. The Rainbow Coalition and Concerned Citizens opposed each other in the election of officers for each precinct. Bishop Willis's organization attempted to oust Mama from her long-held position as committeewoman for Rosemont's Forty-second Precinct. The reason she retained her seat was that elections were held on a precinct-by-precinct basis, meaning that only residents of a precinct could vote for its representative. Willis favored a system where all the attendees present would vote for each open seat. If he flooded the convention with Rainbow Coalition members, they could pick the candidate of their choice in every precinct. Happily for Mama, that time he failed to get his way.

But the rivalry between the bishop and my mother only intensified in 1986. The Rainbow Coalition endorsed Owen Pickett as the Democratic candidate for Congress in the Second District. There was no way Mama was going to endorse Owen Pickett, who was running against Republican Joe Canada. Concerned Citizens endorsed neither.

The Concerned Citizens' poll workers were always paid for handing out flyers at the polls on election day. My mother understood that these people counted on that money, so she told them to campaign for whichever candidate would hire them. Some in the Democratic Party accused her of working for Canada, which she denied. Still, the accusation stuck. Pickett won by a ten-to-one margin in Norfolk's black precincts, and went on to be a congressman for seven terms.

A RUINOUS RIVALRY

In April 1987, *The Virginian-Pilot* published a feature story on the rivalry between my mother and Bishop Willis. He denied any such rivalry existed—which no one believed—and claimed that it was a creation of the news media. By then it was clear that a rivalry had been underway for a good while, and that the bishop was winning. He was chairman of the Second Congressional District Democratic Committee, a position formerly held by my mother. His Rainbow Coalition had eclipsed Concerned Citizens at several elections. Even delegates Billy Robinson and Yvonne Miller had jumped ship to join the Rainbow. In the House of Delegates election that year, Concerned Citizens endorsed neither Democratic incumbent, backing two independent candidates instead—a move which, on the heels of the accusations that she'd backed Joe Canada, placed her squarely in the party's dog house. Both incumbents won easily.

That July, she resigned from her position on the NRHA at the close of her term. Her health was worse than ever: Mama used a wheelchair to get around now. She wanted to devote more time to Concerned Citizens. She wasn't happy with a proposal that would see NRHA disbanded, and its responsibilities assumed by city officials. And she was protesting the agency's treatment of its chairman, Julian Rashkind —his term had expired a year before, and he continued to work for the authority while the question of his reappointment languished. "This is voluntary work," she said. "Here we are, giving our time to the city, and then they don't think enough of us to take any action on Mr. Rashkind's reappointment. . . .That gives me a signal."

The mayor called Mama a "substantial contributor to the redevelopment of the city" who "performed well for the city." George Banks, president of Berkley's Beacon Light Civic

League, regretted her resignation. "She was somebody that citizens could look up to," he told the newspaper. "She was dedicated to people who normally don't have representation."

Her one great regret as a commissioner was the redevelopment of Church Street, the one-time central business district of the black community, now little more than an empty wasteland. Redevelopment's first stage, bulldozing, had gone wonderfully, but the authority had failed to proceed to replacing the vanished businesses that had lined the street. The demolitions had erased black Norfolk's gathering place, its cultural center, its geographic heart. Mama did succeed in convincing the NRHA to donate public land at the intersection of Church Street and Brambleton Avenue for the construction of a Martin Luther King monument, an idea first proposed by Mr. Jordan in 1970.

Then, at the city's Democratic convention in December, the rivalry between Bishop Willis and my mother reached its logical conclusion. He had succeeded in changing the convention rules from precinct-by-precinct voting to at-large voting. Mama was voted out of her position as committeewoman for the Forty-second Precinct. Bill Harris, a former mailman who sold real estate, took her place. She had never even heard his name. A man introduced himself to her when the voting was over, and told her he had always had great admiration for her. She peered up at him from her wheelchair and asked who he was. It was Bill Harris.

The picture accompanying an article about the convention depicts her wearing a tired smile. She told the newspaper she expected to lose, because of the change in rules. "It's no problem," she said. "I'll still be doing the same thing, registering people to vote and still getting people elected."

CHAPTER TWELVE

TWILIGHT AND HONOR

While the primaries for the 1988 presidential election were conducted that spring, the NAACP announced that it planned to protest the presence of the Confederate battle flag on the dais of Norfolk's City Council chambers. Many people did not even realize it was there, because the various flags that had flown over Norfolk over its long history hung furled, and easily overlooked, on poles on the chamber's back wall. But James Gay, now president of the local NAACP, planned to appear before the council and demand the flag's removal. He told associates that he hoped the council would refuse, at which point he'd storm the dais and try to pull down the flag himself—and if a council member tried to stop him, he wouldn't let go. Imagine the scene described in *The Virginian-Pilot*: There'd be Gay struggling with officialdom over the flag. It would make the national news.

But Norfolk was slowly, and somewhat reluctantly, shedding its Jim Crow past. Mayor Joe Leafe ordered the flag removed before the council met. When Gay and other NAACP officers arrived at the chambers for its regular Tuesday meeting, the battle flag was nowhere to be seen.

In April, at the city Democratic caucus, 160 delegates and eighty alternates were selected to attend state and district conventions to be held later in the year. The Rainbow Coalition was not able to recruit 240 people to file for all the delegate spots, so members of Concerned Citizens and a handful of Lyndon LaRouche supporters—backers of a leftist labor economist who campaigned for president in every election from 1976 to 2004—also filed. This produced the slimmest of surpluses: In all, 241 people vied for 240 convention seats. Mama was the only person cut.

Earl Swift of *The Virginian-Pilot* called it a "mean-spirited, low-down, belly-crawling shame." Barbara Hickey, the city Democratic Committee's chairwoman, told the reporter it was retribution for "going against Billy Robinson." The delegate himself, who was not present for the voting, told Swift that he had tried to patch things up with Mama, but had given up. "I owe her a great deal, and look to her as my political mother, and would never do anything knowingly to injure her," Robinson said. "But she has a view of life and of politics, and essentially, it's her way or no way. And that's not conducive to coalition or shared politics." Likewise, Herbert Collins faulted her for not supporting Democratic candidates endorsed by the Rainbow Coalition. They weren't completely right: Concerned Citizens supported Jesse Jackson that year on Super Tuesday, and he was the coalition's founder and national leader.

Mama claimed to be unfazed by the development. She pointed out that Bishop Willis owned two radio stations, but hadn't been able to attract a large enough following to fill the convention. "He wouldn't have taken the LaRouche people, and he wouldn't have gotten my people, if he had all 240 people," she said. She suspected the Rainbow Coalition was not as powerful as some believed.

Time would prove that Mama was not being stubborn or self-destructive or autocratic, as many of her critics said. There was more to the feud than petty competition with Bishop Willis. She believed in standing up to the power structure, in fighting for equality, whether she was fighting a longstanding system that preserved white supremacy, or black men who thought themselves superior to a humble seamstress. You did not underestimate or disrespect Evelyn Butts and get away with it, and she did not have to do anything to diminish her main detractor. Bishop Willis unraveled his power and his reputation all by himself.

The first inkling that something was wrong with Bishop Willis's business empire came in the fall of 1988. Atlantic National Bank was losing money and in trouble with federal regulators over questionable lending practices. The bank's assets were in decline. A teller was investigated for embezzling funds. Bishop Willis was a past president of the bank and the current chairman of its board of directors. He was also its debtor: He owed the bank $201,000. By the end of 1989, federal regulators had shut down the operation, citing illegal and unsound practices. It was reorganized under new management as New Atlantic National Bank.

Bishop Willis's radio empire was also in decline. Crusade for Christ sought a $400,000 loan in the late 1980s from Clarence Britt of Hampton, who was later convicted of cocaine dealing and sentenced to seventeen years in prison. The Internal Revenue Service and the state of Virginia filed liens against some of the bishop's radio stations for unpaid taxes. In 1989, he was forced to sell WOWI-FM to service his debts. He gave up all his state and local Democratic leadership posts. The rainbow was starting to fade.

Bishop Willis's effort to raise money for a long-promised Martin Luther King memorial was plagued by rumors of mismanagement. The bishop turned over fundraising responsibility to Rev. I. Joseph Williams. In 1989, Mr. Jordan assumed control of the project through the tax-exempt Judge Joe Jordan Foundation, and he tapped businesswoman Rosa Alexander to lead the effort.

The bishop's legal and financial problems only deepened. He was required to repay $580,000 to the government for the loan he received from the convicted drug dealer, because the money was alleged to have come from drug proceeds. He repaid an $88,000 loan from a Norfolk State University vice president in increments of less than $10,000, and was accused of trying to skirt reporting laws—a charge on which he'd eventually be sentenced in federal court to four months of house detention.

While the bishop's star fell, Mama enjoyed some small vindication. In May of that same year, she was honored for her lifelong community service by the Norfolk and Portsmouth Bar Association, an organization that had had an all-white membership when she began her political career. She received the prestigious Liberty Bell Award, presented at the association's annual Law Day luncheon to "an individual who promotes a better understanding and appreciation of the rule of law, who encourages a greater respect for law and the courts, who stimulates a sense of civic responsibility, and who contributes to the effectiveness of our institutions of government." The award had never been awarded to a black person.

Mama also received the Martin Luther King Jr. Lifetime Achievement Award in January 1990 from the Hampton Roads Black Media Professionals, during that group's annual Echoes of Excellence awards program.

Around this time, she told longtime Concerned Citizens member Horace Downing that she wanted to retire as chairwoman. In June 1990, he sent a letter to the remaining members of the organization announcing elections for officers. Mama did not attend. In fact, only four people showed up, some of them more than an hour late. They voted to remove Mama as chairwoman and appointed Mr. Downing as acting chairman. The once-powerful organization she had founded, which was the fulcrum of her political influence, was on the skids. "I'm retiring now because my health isn't good," she told *The Virginian-Pilot*. "It's strictly health. I'm not as well as I used to be.

"It's difficult, because there are a lot of things I wanted to do, and a lot of things people still want me to do. People still call me."

She was telling the truth. She'd always been heavy, but now her weight made it hard for her to get around. She developed osteoarthritis in her hip. The hernia that had sent her into emergency surgery in New York continued to cause her intestinal problems. In the final months of her life she required dialysis, not from diabetes, but from the effects of high blood pressure. Though only sixty-three, she looked and felt older.

Organizations continued to honor her. The Oakwood Civic League had given her an award a few days before that sad Concerned Citizens session. When her term expired that summer, Mama resigned from the State Housing and Community Development Board, too.

Concerned Citizens planned to reorganize, to increase membership among eighteen- to thirty-five-year-old voters, and to prepare the community for the advent of a ward system in Norfolk. The lawsuit filed in 1984 to replace Norfolk's at-large system for electing council members had finally been decided after ping-ponging in the federal courts for six years. When the Supreme Court declined to hear the case in 1990, it effectively affirmed the judgment of the Fourth Circuit that at-large elections were discriminatory.

James Gay, the plaintiff who'd said Mama did nothing more than supply lunches in Norfolk elections, was victorious at last. But like the bishop, he was unable to fully enjoy the fruits of his success. The bar found him guilty of mishandling a client's trust fund in 1989, and his license was suspended for three years. In 1990, he was indicted for writing a bad $605 check. That was a felony, and precipitated his resignation from the NAACP.

Now retired, my mother had no meetings to attend, no volunteer obligations to meet, for the first time since World War II. I was back in Germany, but my daughter Evelyn attended Norfolk State from 1987 to 1991, and I was grateful that she could spend time with her grandmother. She loved to stop by for a home-cooked meal. One of her favorites was Mama's fried spots, a fish (*Leiostomus xanthurus*) found in Chesapeake Bay.

Mama was so proud to attend her namesake's NSU graduation in May 1991 at the Scope arena in downtown Norfolk. Evelyn was a psychology major, and graduated cum laude. I flew home from Germany with my husband and youngest daughter,

Robin, to attend the ceremony. The commencement speaker was Jesse Jackson. Most commencement speeches are short and staid. Rev. Jackson's speech was fifty-five minutes long and interrupted frequently by cheers and applause.

Jackson took aim at President George H.W. Bush in his speech, criticizing the White House's proposals for school choice, which promised to benefit only the well-off and to gut public education funding. "If there's to be real choice, people must have the means to choose," he told graduates. "There is no choice in unemployment. There is no choice in poverty. Choice is a code word for exclusion—the exclusion of those students who have no choice by those who have many." At the end of his speech, he received a standing ovation. Mama was exhausted by the ceremony, which lasted three and one-half hours.

***

Nothing confirms more clearly that you are reaching the final phase of life than losing your friends. Mama paid a last visit to her friend, lawyer, political ally, and inspiration, Joe Jordan. He died in June 1991, at age sixty-seven, in the VA Hospital in Hampton, following a battle with liver cancer. Mr. Jordan and my mother would forever be remembered as the team that abolished Virginia's poll tax. He was just six years out of law school when he helped argue the case before the U.S. Supreme Court. "The poll tax symbolized the worst aspects of discrimination and segregation," he once said. "To have lived with the problem, and then have the opportunity to successfully argue against it before the Supreme Court, that was a milestone in my life."

A *The Virginian-Pilot* article memorializing Judge Jordan included the surprising fact that he was censured by the Virginia Supreme Court for violating the constitutional rights of some who appeared before him. He handed out tough sentences and had to defend his courtroom practices before the Judicial Inquiry and Review Commission. "The allegation was that I had violated the rights of defendants, specifically a white woman prostitute, who was trespassing in the Ocean View area," he told historian Tommy Bogger in 1989. "There was a serious problem down there, and continues to be a problem of prostitution, drugs, and what have you. The citizens wanted it dealt with. The courts just didn't deal with it—but I dealt with it."

He explained his judicial philosophy to Bogger in the same conversation. "I felt that you can't have respect for the law unless the law means what it says," he said, "and probably developed a reputation as a hanging judge, as some chose to call me. But I tried to say that no matter who it is that comes before a court, if they are guilty, they are going to get it in a meaningful way." He had no shame about the controversy over his courtroom practices. "I got in trouble with the white community because if whites committed an offense, especially against blacks, they got it too, and that wasn't supposed to happen," he said. "So, the black lawyers were mad with me, and the white lawyers were mad with me, and they did their best to make it difficult for me... I was at ease doing what I felt was right, and I would be there now unless I'd been impeached, but they had not succeeded in that."

Judge Jordan had also earned a name for his treatment of domestic violence cases. "Most of the suffering of black women was crimes committed against them by black men, and in the past, that didn't matter," he told Bogger. "Most black women would come in, after the conflict was over, and withdraw the warrants.

"I felt under duress. You know, you're a six-foot-two man, two hundred pounds, coming into court with a five-foot woman, and she says, 'Everything is all right. I want to drop the warrant.' I never permitted that in my court. I said, 'I'd be glad to consider that after I hear what occurred.' And then I would hear the case. And nine times out of ten, the violation was there, and I would punish the man. And eventually, the ladies began to realize that they could expect a fair resolution of their rights in court, and one of the refreshing things is any day I meet ladies who said, "My God, I wish you were still there. You certainly protected us."

"That's unforgiveable, in my judgment—that if women are less in our society, black women were even less, you see. And somebody had to say, 'Oh, no, no, no.'"

Mama, meanwhile, was not faring well. She had been in and out of the hospital every year since 1989. She had lost some weight, but her health was not improving. In 1992, she did not even have the energy to work on Bill Clinton's presidential campaign. By this time, I was finishing my tour in Germany, and was reassigned to Offutt Air Force Base in Nebraska. When my husband and I changed duty stations, we always visited relatives in Virginia and Kentucky. Although we had enjoyed Germany and our travels in Europe, we couldn't wait to be home again. We had been out of the country for four years.

When we got to Norfolk in October 1992, Mama was in the hospital. She was having transient ischemic attacks, or mini-strokes, so she was in and out of consciousness. One day late in the month, I received a call at Mama's house from Betsy

Phillips, the wife of City Councilman and Republican insider G. Conolly Phillips. "How is Mrs. Butts doing?" she asked me. "We were just over to see her and she said they aren't treating her well."

"They are treating her just fine," I replied. "She is having mini-strokes, and her mind is in and out."

Mrs. Phillips then got down to the meat of her call. "Mrs. Butts told me she would endorse Chuck Griffith for commonwealth's attorney in the upcoming election," she said, referring to a Republican candidate for the city's top law enforcement position. "I would like for you to call Mrs. Butts's poll workers together, so we can have a meeting at her house." I told Mrs. Phillips that I would get back to her the next day.

Later that evening I went over to the hospital to visit my mother and I asked her if she had agreed to endorse Chuck Griffith and to have a meeting at her house. She said she had not. When I spoke to Mrs. Phillips the next day, I informed her with all the politeness I could muster, "I am not calling a meeting to organize workers for Chuck Griffith."

Mrs. Phillips apparently did not like my response and she hotly replied, "I am going to call a reporter at *The Virginian-Pilot* and tell him that Evelyn Butts's daughter would not let her will be done. She will not let her endorse Chuck Griffith."

"Evelyn Butts is a Democrat," I told her, "and Chuck Griffith is a Republican, and the presidential election is too important to send the signal to vote Republican." And with that, our conversation was done, though I knew the matter was not.

I immediately dispatched my husband to the hospital, because I worried they would go there to try to pressure Mama while she was in her weakened state of health. I was right. The candidate himself was surprised to see my husband at the hospital. He asked who he was, and Robert replied, "Her son." Mr. Griffith shot back that Mrs. Butts didn't have a son. Robert clarified that he was her son-in-law. Mr. Griffith left the premises, but he gave Robert a five-paragraph letter for my mother written on campaign stationery. "It appears that your daughter objects to your support of me for her own personal reasons," the letter read. "It is unfortunate that she has taken such a position, but I do not want to contribute to any stress that the situation may place upon you." He closed the letter by expressing his "hope that your daughter's actions in interfering with your decision to assist me does not contribute to a bad result." He wished her a speedy recovery and promised to visit her when she returned home.

I had to wonder if these people were trying to get me to contact the newspaper so they could get more publicity—imagine the fuss that would have erupted over a lifelong Democratic activist not only endorsing a Republican candidate, but hosting a support event at her home! Later that day, when Robert returned from the hospital with the letter and Mama's car, I visited Mr. Phillips at his auto dealership on Military Highway. I asked him and his wife to leave my family alone—no more calls or letters. I thought then, and still think today, that they exhibited a total disregard for my mother. Chuck Griffith won without her support, by the way.

I had no choice but to leave Virginia and report to Offutt Air Force Base. Because of her high blood pressure, Mama began dialysis after her discharge from the hospital. A friend and longtime political ally, Claude Stevens, drove her to the medical center. He used to joke that he was "Driving Miss Daisy."

She did not seem to have a recurrence of mini-strokes, but was depressed about having to undergo dialysis. Thank God for Joe, the disabled veteran living in Mama's house. A home health aide and housekeeper who took care of him, Mildred, kept us informed of Mama's condition. In January, Mama was well enough to fly with my sister Jeanette to California. She stayed there for more than a month. Mildred slept at Mama's house to look after Joe. Jeanette brought Mama home in March 1993, and stayed a few days. One morning shortly after she returned to California, Mildred checked on Mama and found that she had died in her sleep.

Mama's sisters Bunky, Pudney, and Rosanna came over to the house to say goodbye to their big sister, and to phone the news to family and friends. Mama was the first of the sisters to pass away. My brother-in-law, Jimmie, gave me the news before 6 a.m. I think Jeanette was too upset to call. She'd just seen Mama, and had not seen the end coming. Mama had seemed fine when Jeanette left for home. Tired, but certainly not dying.

There was a bitter winter chill in the air in Bellevue, the town south of Omaha where Offutt Air Force Base is located. We were living in a basement apartment while we waited for a house to be built. I just wanted to get out of Nebraska and go home. I was stunned that my mother had died. My daughter Evelyn and her husband were staying with us, on their way to Tinker Air Force Base in Oklahoma. Robert, Evelyn and I left for Virginia the next morning by car. I thought I was being logical in picking our route, but in hindsight, I have to admit that I was not thinking straight. I did not want to drive through

Chicago on Interstate 80, so we went south to Kansas City and picked up Interstate 70, which meets Interstate 64 in St. Louis. We planned to take I-64 all the way to Norfolk.

Around Louisville, Kentucky, it started to snow. We decided to head farther south to avoid the mountains of West Virginia, but I never bothered to check the weather forecast—we just assumed the weather would improve as we drove south. By the time we got to Nashville, it was evening. We could not find a hotel room, and the weather kept getting worse, so we continued south on Interstate 65—until the winter storm stopped traffic on the interstate, marooning us in the car for hours. When traffic finally started moving, we made it to Birmingham, Alabama, where we slept on a firehouse floor with about fifty other travelers. Somehow, the three of us took it in stride. I now see that long journey as a metaphor: Your mother dies, and you find yourself horribly lost in a storm.

We finally arrived in Norfolk after seventy-two hours of travel. We made funeral arrangements with Mr. Graves, one of Mama's longtime fellow activists, whose funeral home was one of the few commercial businesses on the redeveloped Church Street. He suggested having the funeral four days later, on a Friday. The house was full all week. My sisters Patricia and Jeanette came from California with their children and grandchildren. We knew we would have to make arrangements for Joe, who had lived in my mother's house for thirteen years. Aunt Bunky told him he could stay with her, and he wound up living in her house until he died.

Earl Swift had written a piece in *The Virginian-Pilot* the day after Mama died. He ended it with a lament about her disappearance from public life. "When I heard that she died Thursday, I couldn't help but feel frustrated," he wrote. "This was someone who should have finished life celebrated, rather than forgotten. She took a righteous fight to the U.S. Supreme Court, and persevered until she won. She commanded the city's most powerful political machine at a time when women, especially black women, didn't lead squat. She gave practically every black leader in Norfolk his or her political start. She signed up the tens of thousands of voters who have put those blacks in power.

"History better be kind to this woman. Evelyn Butts was important."

There was a steady stream of visitors to her house all week. Everyone brought food until there wasn't room in the refrigerator or on the counters. The funeral was going to be held at First Church of Christ Holiness on Princess Anne Road in uptown Norfolk. A news station called to ask whether it could record the service inside the church. We consented.

I was dreading the sight of my mother in her casket. We went to the funeral home to view her privately sometime that week. It was just my sisters and me. Patricia and Jeanette had the courage to approach the casket to touch her and say goodbye. I couldn't do it. I cried from a distance.

On Thursday night, there was a wake at the Oakwood Chapel Church of Christ in our old neighborhood. Being on time was ingrained in me, thanks to my military career, and I was ready long before my sisters. We were late to the service, but I was relieved that no one seemed to notice. On the back of the program, we printed words written by Mama, probably from her campaign literature.

The only way we can succeed is to. . .

Fight for what we believe in

Reach out to each other with love

Never forget our ancestors and what they achieved

Be courageous and innovative in all our doing

Register to vote

Vote

Labor hard for the betterment of our people

Be concerned for our community

Invent solutions for the future

Direct knowledge through intelligence

Encourage our young, they are our future

Love one another, for God is love

Walk with dignity and respect of each other

That Friday, Mr. Graves sent limousines to Mama's house to pick us up. He told us we were not to be late, and I played the role of drill sergeant to get my sisters ready on time. We had a police escort from Mama's house to the church. Hundreds of people came to pay their respects, including U.S. Representative Bobby Scott, state senators Yvonne Miller and Louise Lucas, Delegate Kenneth Melvin, Norfolk Mayor Mason Andrews, and City Councilman Joe Green.

The pews were filled with political aspirants, black and white, whom Mama had supported. The service lasted about an hour. Bishop O.W. McInnis delivered her eulogy. My friend Gwendolyn Robinson came from Washington D.C. to sing. Reverend Green and Senator Miller also spoke. I can't remember much of what they said, because I was focused on my sister Patricia. She was upset about the way Mama had been treated in the last years of her political career, and she made comments under her breath throughout the service. I think it was in that moment that the seeds of this book were born.

The ceremony underlined for me that whatever her failings, Mama's legacy would be lasting. She lived on in a landmark U.S. Supreme Court case, in the brick-and-mortar buildings and projects she helped create, and in the minds and memories of her fellow citizens. Almost twenty-five years after that funeral, I would find myself conducting research at Norfolk's Slover Memorial Library. When I mentioned her name to the staff, it made me proud to hear the reference librarian say, "I am a great admirer of your mother." Later, I stopped a bus displaying a destination sign that read "Evelyn Butts" and asked the driver if she would idle the vehicle long enough for me to take a picture. She asked, "Who was she?" I am always filled with pride to say, "She was my mother."

The police escorted us to Forest Lawn Cemetery, and Mama was laid to rest alongside our father. The police escorted funeral cars back to the church for a repast, then waited to escort the family limousine back to Mama's house. Mr. Graves told us that he'd never seen them do that.

The Virginian-Pilot and J*ournal and Guide* wrote about the funeral. The *Journal* called her the "Mother of Norfolk Politics." Councilman Paul Riddick told the paper she'd "single-handedly helped transform the political process of Norfolk to make it a useful tool for black empowerment." No one had, or would, "equal her role and ability to mobilize the masses to vote and make an impact on an election," he said. "For two decades, the white political bosses of the city knew that Evelyn Butts was the one who decided who got the massive amount of votes in the city."

The story also covered the rift between the Rainbow Coalition and Concerned Citizens, offering up the conventional wisdom that Mama and Bishop Willis should have teamed up, but were prevented from doing so by their personal disagreements. A longtime supporter and friend of Mama's told the newspaper that the rift hurt her deeply. "We deserved much more at that time," she said, "and I think history will say that she, above the politicians and the power brokers, helped push Norfolk and the country forward in terms of civil rights by assuring that each of us had equal access to the ballot."

Senator Miller summarized Mama's career nicely when I interviewed her in October 2007. "She was a person who had very strong principles," she told me. "She was not impressed by people's titles and positions. She was concerned about the people at the bottom. And she worked very hard to help them understand the process. And to register them to vote. And to turn out votes. Nobody since her has been able to do that kind of registering of people or to turn out that kind of vote. Or to keep the cohesion in the community as long as she kept it. She was thought of as the mother of the community. A lot of people respected her."

My sisters and I lingered in Norfolk for three weeks to dispose of Mama's furniture and belongings. We made sure we saved all the personal papers and newspaper clippings from her life's work. I wanted to keep her bedroom suite, and Jeanette took the dining room table and chairs. Patricia flew home to California. My sister Jeanette and her husband, Jimmie, drove a rented truck with me to Nebraska, and from there they continued on to California. We fearlessly drove through Chicago this time, and laughed about the wandering, snow-blinded journey of just a month before. It was April now, and the weather was lovely.

EPILOGUE

I'd like to think she was there in spirit, with her arms stretched wide, beaming her gap-toothed smile, welcoming home her prodigal sons. On May Day 1994, a little more than two years after Mama died, many of her political children gathered for a press conference at City Hall to announce that they were leaving the Rainbow Coalition to return to Concerned Citizens. Billy Robinson was there. Vice Mayor Paul Riddick was there. Even her old foe Herbert Collins, who'd run against Mama for City Council in 1982 as a Rainbow candidate, attended.

James Rivers, president of Concerned Citizens, expressed no animosity toward Bishop Willis or the Rainbow, but he plainly described the quandary facing those gathered. "Here we have a convicted felon trying to lead a politically active organization in one of the largest cities in Virginia," he said. "Such people usually lose their right to vote. Thus, it undermines the political and organizational structure of any political effort."

If Mama was looking down on the event, I'm confident she was neither gloating nor bitter, but simply enjoying the thing she loved most—fighting injustice, and eventually winning. The sixth lesson I could impart from the life of Evelyn T. Butts is this: Never try to win approval from someone who thinks you are inferior. Prove them wrong, yes. But, never compromise your principles over someone who thinks they are better than you because of gender, education, wealth, or anything else.

Not long after she died, Mama's friend Claude Stevens (Driving Miss Daisy) suggested to Herbert Collins—who'd finally won a council seat under the ward system he fought to create—that a street in Oakwood be renamed Evelyn T. Butts Avenue. Councilman Collins sponsored the measure, and it passed overwhelmingly. Mr. Stevens told the *Journal and Guide* that the street should serve not only as a tribute to Evelyn Butts, but to "all women who were not well-educated, who were domestics and mothers, who were the backbone of their family and community, who loved their people so much they were the ones who stood up when others refused to, because they selfishly thought they had too much to lose."

Mr. Stevens was from the rough neighborhood of Bedford-Stuyvesant in New York City. He worked on Shirley Chisholm's congressional campaign before moving to Norfolk in the early 1970s. He clearly felt great love and support for strong black women. "Once, Oakwood was nothing more than a set of houses sitting along muddy unpaved streets with septic tanks and outhouses," he told the *Journal and Guide.* "But because of the work and persistence of Mrs. Butts, it was brought to a respectable level by the city."

Our neighbor Mr. Herbert Smith agreed, saying Mama "saved this neighborhood out here.

"The city put us on the demolition list," he said. "She went around and got people to upgrade their bathrooms to get hooked into the city's water system. Then she went down to City Hall and stayed in their faces until they agreed." His son, Andrew

Smith, called her "a great role model for us" who would "always fight for us.

"She was right there in the neighborhood doing these things. We could actually see her working. It gave us all a sense that you can fight City Hall, and that you can win."

On a research trip to Norfolk while I was writing this book, somebody told me that there was a photograph of my mother in the Norview Community Center. She had been instrumental in getting the original community center built while she was on the NRHA board. I learned that her friend Mrs. Marie Young was responsible for putting Mama's picture and a plaque in a glass display case in the new building when the old one was demolished and rebuilt. The plaque reads, "For the dedication of her time and passion to the community."

There are so many things in Norfolk that remind me of her. When I drive by Waterside, I think of her. When I pass the Martin Luther King obelisk, finally erected in 2000 at the intersection of Church and Brambleton, I think of her. A mural on the side of a building near the intersection of Thirty-fifth Street and Colonial Avenue includes images of Mama and Mr. Jordan; his office was once inside. Even Norfolk State University reminds me of her. As Senator Miller said in our 2007 interview, "There is nobody in this city that has done more to help people than Mrs. Butts. I don't think the people at Norfolk State understand how much she worked to get the land they needed from the Redevelopment and Housing Authority."

In 2000, *The Virginian-Pilot* picked "Twenty Tidewater Titans" of the twentieth century, people who deserved the credit or blame for the way Norfolk had come to be. Among white millionaires and captains of industry such as Charles Kaufman,

Walter Chrysler and Joseph Taussig, the three black titans chosen to be on the list were Mama, Mr. Jordan, and the early publisher of the *Journal and Guide*, P.B. Young. Mama was the only woman.

If you have reached this point in this story, you know my mother was a Democrat, and you know that she believed in voting. Today, we Democrats have lost our belief in the franchise. When election day comes around, we stay home. It would make my mother proud if this book could begin to change that.

The public has forgotten how effective the poll tax was in diluting democracy. The legislation that established poll taxes included no words that signaled discrimination against blacks, yet the intention of the authors was well known. Today, voter suppression is achieved through strict voter ID laws. On its face, proving identity appears to be a reasonable idea, yet voter ID laws disenfranchise thousands of poor people in each election. Thurgood Marshall's turnstile where voters have to pay to vote has been moved to the Department of Motor Vehicles licensing centers. In Alabama, the state denies ex-felons the right to vote until they have paid all fines, court costs and financial obligations to victims. The idea, expressed in *Harper v. Virginia Bd. of Elections*, that a "State violates the Equal Protection Clause of the Fourteenth Amendment whenever it makes the affluence of the voter or payment of any fee an electoral standard," has been eclipsed by current voter eligibility laws. I hope this book will invigorate the fight to abolish laws that result in voter suppression.

Still, some people decline to vote because they believe there's little difference between the two major parties. I can hear my mother say, "Oh, please." Democrats stand for equal justice, for women's rights, for the economically downtrodden. You can thank Democrats for Social Security, Medicare, and the Voting Rights Act. Don't you dare tell me that there's no difference.

Others stay home because they believe politics is corrupt and dirty. If my mother could, I know she'd say this: "If you don't vote, you can be assured that corrupt politicians will be elected." Which leads to the seventh and final lesson to be taken from my mother's life. All public figures have enemies. Some enemies are earned, and some are attracted by power and influence, as moths to a flame. It's true that your enemies can take you out of the game. But you must never let the dirtiness of politics keep you on the sidelines. Never fail to fight.

With the benefit of hindsight, it is indisputable that my mother's downfall came about because of the actions of several black male ministers. Her own people! I honestly don't know what lesson can be drawn from that.

In the 1980s, the word "intersectionality" was not in our collective vocabulary, but my mother perfectly illustrates the concept. She was black. She was a woman. She was poor. She had dropped out of high school. She was overweight and she spoke loudly with confidence in her opinions in a voice that disclosed her working-class, almost rural upbringing. But, this large, black poor woman was in the room with politically powerful white people, making policy and advocating for the poor, and it drove some suit-wearing, educated, well-heeled, middle-class, male ministers nuts. Some wanted her place. Or, they believed her place should be subordinate to a man. Mr. Jordan,

Mr. Dawley and Mr. Holt had never treated her like she was inferior, and she had no idea how to deal with it.

When her public career ended, my mother retreated to private life and to the role she assumed in fifth grade when her mother died: Mama. She occupied her time by being a mother, a grandmother, a caregiver, a homemaker and a fantastic cook. To say that her post-political years were tragic is to miss how much strength and satisfaction she drew from those roles. She may have retreated, but she was not defeated.

We will never come to consensus on why Evelyn Butts lost her political power. I believe she would have been elected in 1980 if Concerned Citizens had put her name alone on the Goldenrod ballot and encouraged black voters to "single shot" vote for her. I believe she would have won in 1982 if James Gay and Herbert Collins had not run against her. However, there will always be people in Norfolk who thought her "style" made her unelectable, that she brought about her own demise by being stubborn or autocratic. Whatever her failings, her legacy is not in dispute. She will always exist in the pages of a U.S. Supreme Court case, in brick and mortar buildings that she helped to create, and in the memories of people she never met. For me, her last surviving daughter, Evelyn Butts will always be a great American hero.

Now, go vote!

ACKNOWLEDGMENTS

This book would not have been possible without the extraordinary support of a number of people. I have to begin with my husband, Robert, who provided me with emotional support throughout the writing process, and provided me with guidance on the direction of the story.

I am forever grateful to my sister Jeanette, and brother-in-law, Jimmie Brinkley, whose limitless support made this book possible. I also want to thank my collaborator, Kietryn Zychal, for helping me shape my own memories, a mountain of press clippings, hours of oral interviews, and a jumble of historical data, into what I hope is an informative and interesting book.

Thank you to Earl Swift, my editor, who has been invaluable. Thank you, too, to Rodney Jordan, who was a great source of historical data and continues to be a font of support. Thank You to Mayor Kenneth Cooper Alexander for his contribution.

I could not be more grateful to Peg O'Dea Lippert, who encouraged me at every stage of writing this book. She took the time to read my drafts, and offered comments that made this a much better book. Thank you to Michael Knepler who took the time to read and provide helpful comments on my draft. I owe a special thanks to Alveta Green, Walter Green, Senator Yvonne Miller, Ellis James, Yvonne Merritt, former Virginia governor and former US senator Chuck Robb and all the people that took the time to talk with me about Mama.

I also thank Norfolk State University for the use of the Harrison B. Wilson Archives. I'm especially grateful to Dr. Tommy Bogger and Annette Montgomery for their contributions and support.

Maureen Watts, a research librarian for *The Virginian-Pilot*, offered invaluable help. Finally, the staff of the Norfolk Public Library's Sargeant Memorial Collection was extremely helpful and cordial every time I visited that wonderful facility. Thank you, all.

ENDNOTES

Chapter One

The Weather Company, "Washington DC, January 25, 1966."
Wunderground.com. 2017. Web. 4 April 2017. https://www.
wunderground.com/history

Virginia Senate Resolution no. 106 on the death of Evelyn T. Butts. 7
Apr 1993.

Bogger, Dr. Tommy. "History of Norfolk Project. Oral Interview of
Mrs Evelyn Butts." July 26, 1989.

"Brown v. Board of Education of Topeka: The Case of the Century."
Kansasmemory.org. Kansas Historical Society, 2007-2017. Web. 18
May 2017. http://www.kansasmemory.org/item/224239/text

Chapter Two

Fausz, J. Frederick. "Powhatan Uprising of 1622." Historynet.
com. World History Group, 2017. Web. 17 April 2017. http://www.
historynet.com/powhatan-uprising-of-1622.htm

Rein, Lisa. "Mystery of Va. First Slaves Unlocked 400 Years Later."
Washington Post. 3 September 2006. http://www.washingtonpost.
com/wp-dyn/content/article/2006/09/02/AR2006090201097.html

"Britain in the New World. The House of Burgesses." Ushistory.org. U.S. History Online Textbook. 2017. Web. 17 April 2017. http://www. ushistory.org/us/2f.asp

"The Growth of Slavery." Ushistory.org. U.S. History Online Textbook. 2017. Web. 17 April 2017. http://www.ushistory.org/us/6c.asp

Erickson, Mark St. John. "Civil War at 150: Lincoln directs fall of Norfolk." Daily Press Media Group, 2012. Web. 17 April 2017. http:// articles.dailypress.com/2012-05-05/features/dp-nws-surrender-of-norfolk-20120505_1_gosport-navy-yard-lincoln-fort-monroe

Smith, T. L. "Oakwood School Reunion." *Journal and Guide*, Jul 18, 1984, pp. 4,

History.com Staff. "Battle of Hampton Roads." History.com. A+E Networks, 2017. Web. 17 April 2017. http://www.history.com/topics/ american-civil-war/battle-of-hampton-roads

Littlejohn, Jeffrey L. "Slavery Virginia Timeline." Studythepast. com. Jeffrey L. Littlejohn, 2016. Web. 17 April 2017. http://www. studythepast.com/slaveryvirginiatimeline.pdf

"10 Facts: The Emancipation Proclamation." Civilwar.org. Civil War Trust, 2017. Web. 17 April 2017. http://www.civilwar.org/education/ history/emancipation-150/10-facts.html?referrer=https://www.google. com/

Eaton, Lorraine. "Retracing the steps of slavery in Hampton Roads." *The Virginian-Pilot*. 6 February 2009. Web. 17 April 2017. http:// pilotonline.com/guides/african-american-today/retracing-the-steps-of-slavery-in-hampton-roads/article_635485d6-e677-55a9-89a4-1a2c34d02014.html

"The Guilded Age." Ushistory.org. U.S. History Online Textbook, 2017. Web. 17 April 2017. http://www.ushistory.org/us/36.asp

Chapter Three

ENDNOTES

Jeffrey L. Littlejohn and Charles H. Ford. Elusive Equality: Desegregation and Resegregation in Norfolk Public Schools. Charlottesville: University of Virginia Press, 2012.

White, Forrest R. Pride and Prejudice: School Desegregation and Urban Renewal in Norfolk, 1950-1959. Westport, Conn: Praeger, 1992

"'In the Best American Tradition of Freedom, We Defy You': The Radical Partnership of Joseph Jordan, Leonard Holt, and Edward Dawley," The Virginia Forum, Washington and Lee University, Lexington Virginia, March 25, 2011.

"Television News of the Civil Rights Era 1950-1970. Gray Commission." vcdh.virginia.edu. William G. Thomas, III and Rector and Board of Visitors, University of Virginia, 2005. Web. 5.18.2017. http://www2.vcdh.virginia.edu/civilrightstv/glossary/topic-009.html

Bogger, Dr. Tommy. "History of Norfolk Project. Oral Interview of Judge Joseph Jordan." May 31, 1989.

Garwood, Darrell. "Dual System's End To Be Set By Court." *Journal and Guide*, May 22, 1954 page 1. page C1

"Brown v. Board of Education of Topeka: The Case of the Century." Kansasmemory.org. Kansas Historical Society, 2007-2017. Web. 18 May 2017. http://www.kansasmemory.org/item/224239/text

"A Look Back at Brown v. Board of Education." blogs.kentlaw.itt.edu. Illinois Institute of Technology, Chicago College of Law. 16 May 2014. Web. 18 May 2017. http://blogs.kentlaw.iit.edu/iscotus/a-look-back-at-brown-v-board-of-education/

Mitchell, Francis H. "Coronado Bomber Scores on 2nd Try: County Officials Lax on Coronado." *Journal and Guide*. 4 September 1954. C:17

"Coronado Must Have Full Police Protection" *Journal and Guide*, Sep 11, 1954, pg 1

"Coronado: FAMILY FIRED ON Couple Escapes Latest Attack Dusk to Dawn", *Journal and Guide*, Sep 25, 1954 pg1

Civil Rights in U.S and Virginia History. Documents of U.S. Senator Harry F. Byrd. http://www2.vcdh.virginia.edu/reHIST604/images/1954byrd.jpg

Chapter Four

Old Dominion University Digital Collections "School Desegregation in Norfolk Virginia". Web. 21 May 2017 http://dc.lib.odu.edu/cdm/search/searchterm/School%20Desegregation/field/relatii/mode/all/conn/and/order/nosort

Heinemann, R. L. "Harry F. Byrd (1887–1966)." Encyclopedia Virginia. Virginia Foundation for the Humanities, 22 Jun. 2014. Web. 18 May 2017. http://www.encyclopediavirginia.org/Byrd_Harry_Flood_Sr_1887-1966

Tarter, Brent. "Bryd Organization." Encyclopedia Virginia. Virginia Foundation for the Humanities, 7 April 2011. Web. 18 May 2017. http://www.encyclopediavirginia.org/byrd_organization

Poston, Charles E. "Virginia's initial reactions to the Brown v. Board of Education decision." scholarship.richmond.edu. University of Richmond Scholarship Repository. 1967. Web. 18 May 2017. http://scholarship.richmond.edu/cgi/viewcontent.cgi?article=1686&context=honors-theses

Neff, David Pembroke. "The Defenders of State Sovereignty and Individual Liberties." Encyclopedia Virginia. Virginia Foundation for the Humanities, 23 October 2013. Web. 18 May 2017. http://www.encyclopediavirginia.org/Defenders_of_State_Sovereignty_and_Individual_Liberties

Chapter Five

"Group Restrained: Court Halts Picketing At Norfolk Supermarket." *Journal and Guide*; Jan 30, 1960; pg. 4

"Injunction Stands: Case To Be Tried." *Journal and Guide*; Feb 6, 1960; pg. B1

"Many Witnesses Are Heard: Pickets Curbed At Norfolk Market." *Journal and Guide*; Mar 19, 1960

"Picket Plan Not Mine- Robertson: NAACP Head Has 3 Lawyers Enjoined From Using Name." *Journal and Guide*; Aug 19, 1961; pg. B1

"No Radical" – Robertson: Norfolk, NAACP Branch Sets election March 13." *Journal and Guide*; Mar 4, 1961; pg. B1

"Foreman Field Racial Barriers Are Toppled." *Journal and Guide*, Sep 2, 1961; pg. B1

"Highlights of Colts' Win." *Journal and Guide*; Sep 9, 1961; pg. 17

"Says Game Integrated, But: Robertson Warns Against "Purchasing Segregation."" *Journal and Guide*; Aug 26, 1961; pg. C1

""No Radical" – Robertson: Norfolk NAACP Branch Sets Election March 13." *Journal and Guide*; Mar 4, 1961; pg. B1

"Mrs. Butts Screams 'Fix' In Va. NAACP Election." Herald Dispatch; Apr 15, 1961;

"Attack on Courthouse Segregation Came As A Surprise To Norfolk Lawyers." *Journal and Guide*; Apr 20, 1957; pg. 14

"Federal Court Declines To Upset Jim Crow Toilets." *Journal and Guide*; Mar 08, 1958; pg. 10

"Courthouse Race Signs Just 'Invitations' City Says." *Journal and Guide*; Jun 08, 1957

"Gets Hotel Room: Lawyer In 'Sleep In' At John Marshall, Richmond." *Journal and Guide*; Jul 15, 1961

"Norfolk Lawyer Tells Why He Launched His "Renaissance Crusade." *Journal and Guide*; Sep 20, 1958

Butts, Evelyn. "Letter to Fellow NAACP Members." Mar 9, 1961

Chapter Six

Jackson, Luther Porter Negro Office Holders in Virginia 1865-1895. Norfolk, Va., Guide Quality Press, 1945 c. 1946.

Anzalone, Christopher A. Supreme Court Cases on Political Representation 1787-2001. London and New York: Routledge, 2002

McAllister, Bill. "Va. Poll Tax Killed by Court. Victor Expects Another Fight." *The Virginian-Pilot* 25 March 1966.

Littlejohn, Jeffrey L. "The Radical Partnership of Joseph Jordan, Leonard Holt, and Edward Dawley." The Virginia Forum, Washington and Lee University, Lexington Virginia, March 25, 2011.

"Death of Democracy." *Journal and Guide*, Feb 15, 1958, pp. 8

"Votemobile used in Norfolk Drive." *Journal and Guide*, Mar 28, 1959, pp. 1,

"Biggest Turnouts Uptown." *Journal and Guide*, Nov 07, 1959, pp. 1,

Brown v. Suttles, Tax Collector, 383 U.S. 277 (1937)

Butler v. Thompson, 97 F.Supp. 17.22 (1951) aff'd per curiam 341 U.S. 937

U.S. Const. Art. 1, Sec. 2.

"White Voters Suffering from "Blank Sheet" Law." *Journal and Guide*, Apr 15, 1961, pp. 1,

"Three Buses to Washington." *Journal and Guide*, Aug 31, 1963, pp. 2,

"Officers of Norfolk Branch of SCLC Hold Session." Journal and Guide, Nov 09, 1963, pp. 1,

Lyndon B. Johnson: "Address Before a Joint Session of the Congress.," November 27, 1963. Online by Gerhard Peters and John T. Woolley,The American Presidency Project. http://www.presidency.ucsb.edu/ws/?pid=25988.

Mount, Steve. "Ratification of Constitutional Amendments." USConstitution.net. 3 Jan. 2011. Web. 3 April 2016.

Harman v. Forssenius, 380 U.S. 528, 1965

Lewis, Tyler. "Today in Civil Rights History: The 24th Amendment Prohibits Poll Taxes." Civilrights.org. 23 January 2009. Web. 3 April 2017

History.com staff. "Reconstruction." History.com. A+E Networks. 2009. Web. 3 April 2017 http://www.history.com/topics/american-civil-war/reconstruction

Parramore, Thomas C., Stewart, Peter C., Bogger, Tommy L., Norfolk The First Four Centuries. Charlottesville and London: University Press of Virginia, 1994.

Wharton, V. L. "The Race Issue in the Overthrow of Reconstruction in Mississippi: A Paper Read before the American Historical Association, 1940." Phylon (1940-1956), vol. 2, no. 4, 1941, pp. 362–370. JSTOR, JSTOR, www.jstor.org/stable/271241.

Tarter, Brent. "Poll Tax." Encyclopedia Virginia. Virginia Foundation for the Humanities, 2 Jul. 2014. Web. 3 April 2017. http://www.encyclopediavirginia.org/poll_tax#its1

Kirshenbaum, Andrew. "The Injustice of the Poll Tax and Why It Took a Constitutional Amendment to Stop It." Archive.fairvote.org. May 2005. Web. 3 April 2017.

"Reports of the Proceedings and Debates of the Constitutional Convention State of Virginia. June 12, 1901 to June 26, 1902. Volume II." Richmond, Virginia. The Hermitage Press. 1906. https://archive.org/details/reportofproceedi21virg Virginia Constitution, Sec. 18

Ackerman, Bruck and Nou, Jennifer. "Canonizing the Civil Rights Revolution: The People and the Poll Tax." Chicago: Northwestern University Law Review. 2009.

Podolefsky, Ronnie L. "The Illusion of Suffrage: Female Voting Rights and the Women's Poll Tax Repeal Movement After the Nineteenth Amendment." New York City: Columbia Journal of Gender and Law. 1998

David S. Bogen, "The Privileges and Immunities Clause of Article IV." Cleveland. 37 Cas. W. Res. L. Rev. 794 .1987. http://scholarlycommons.law.case.edu/caselrev/vol37/iss4/8

Chapter Seven

Manaker, Richard G. "FDR's Court-Packing Plan: A Study in Irony." Gilderlehrman.org. New York: History Now: The Journal of the Gilder Lehrman Institute. Web. 4 April 2017. https://www.gilderlehrman. org/history-by-era/new-deal/essays/fdr%E2%80%99s-court-packing-plan-study-irony

Millhiser, Ian. "In Defense of Court-Packing." Slate.com. 23 February 2015. Web. 4 April 2017. http://www.slate.com/articles/news_and_ politics/jurisprudence/2015/02/fdr_court_packing_plan_obama_ and_roosevelt_s_supreme_court_standoffs.html

"Civil Rights Act of 1957." Major Acts of Congress. Encyclopidia.com. Web. 4 Apr. 2017.

Mrs. Evelyn Butts, Plaintiff v. Albertis Harrison, et al., Defendants. Civil Action 4460. United States District Court for the Eastern District of Virginia. November 29, 1963. National Archives, Philadelphia.

Kurland, Philip B. and Casper, Gerhard. Landmark Briefs and Arguments of the Supreme Court of the United States: Constitutional Law. Vol. 62. Arlington, Va.: University Publications of America, In., 1975.

"Suit Filed to Contest Poll Tax Law in Virginia." *Washington Post*. 30 November 1963. D1

ProQuest Historical Newspapers: Norfolk *Journal and Guide*. *Journal and Guide*, Dec 7, 1963; pg. 1 (Front page)

Tarter, Brent."Evelyn Thomas Butts (1924-1993)". Dictionary of Virginia Biography. Encyclopedia Virginia. Virginia Foundation for the Humanities, 2 Nov. 2015. Web. 4 Apr. 2017.

Robertson, Nan. "24th Amendment Becomes Official: Johnson Hails Anti-Poll Tax Document at Ceremonies." *The New York Times*, Feb. 5, 1964. pg. A 14

History.com staff. "Slain Civil Rights Workers Found." History.com. A+E Networks. 2010. Web 4 April 2017. http://www.history.com/this-day-in-history/slain-civil-rights-workers-found

Kenworthy, E.W. "President Signs Civil Rights Bill: Bids All Back It." *The New York Times*. 3 July 1964. Web. 4 April 2017. https://partners.nytimes.com/library/national/race/070364race-ra.html

Minore, Jack, Sain, Ramona and Neithercut, Jean. "Through the Years with the GCBA. A Centennial Historical Overview. 1897 – 1997." Gcbalaw.org. Flint, Michigan. 2006. Web. 4 April 2017. http://www.gcbalaw.org/page.cfm?pageid=32

Annie E. Harper et al., Plaintiffs, v. Virginia State Board of Elections et al., Defendants. Mrs. Evelyn Butts, Plaintiff, v. Albertis Harrison, Governor, et al., Defendants. 240 F. Sup. 270 (1964).

Chapter Eight

Civ. A. Nos. 3253, 3346. United States District Court E.D. Virginia, at Alexandria. Argued October 21, 1964. Decided November 10, 1964.

Harper v. Virginia Bd. of elections 383 U.S. 663 (1966)

Peters, Gerhard and Woolley, John T. "Election of 1964." The American Presidency Project. Presidency.ucsb.edu. 1999-2017. Web. 4 April 2017. http://www.presidency.ucsb.edu/showelection.php?year=1964

"Other 63 -- no Title." *Journal and Guide*, Nov 21, 1964, pp. 1,

Klein, Christopher. "Remembering Selma's "Bloody Sunday." History. com. 6 March 2015. Web. 4 April 2017. http://www.history.com/ news/selmas-bloody-sunday-50-years-ago

Peters, Gerhard and Woolley, John T. "Lyndon B. Johnson. Special Message to Congress. March 15, 1965." The American Presidency Project. Presidency.ucsb.edu. 1999-2017. Web. 4 April 2017. http:// www.presidency.ucsb.edu/ws/?pid=26805

Harman v. Forssenius, 380 U.S. 528 (1965).

Voting Rights Act of 1965, Pub. L. No. 89-110, §10, 79 Stat. 437, 442-43 (codified as amended at 42 U.S.C. §1973(b) (2000)).

Graves, John William. "Poll Tax." Encyclopedia of Arkansas. 7 July 2012. Web. 4 April 2017. http://www.encyclopediaofarkansas.net/ encyclopedia/entry-detail.aspx?entryID=5045

Supreme Court of the United States. "The Court and Its Procedures." Supremecourt.gov. 20 March 2017. Web. 4 April 2017. https://www. supremecourt.gov/about/procedures.aspx

The Weather Company, "Norfolk, Virginia. March 25, 1966." Wunderground.com. 2017. Web. 4 April 2017. https://www. wunderground.com/history

Hearst, Joseph. "Robt. Kennedy Urges Voiding of Poll Taxes." Chicago Tribune 16 March 1962: F 9. http://archives.chicagotribune. com/1962/03/16/page/57/article/robt-kennedy-urges-voiding-of-poll-taxes

IIT Chicago Kent College of Law. "Justices." Oyez.org. Web. 4 April 2017. https://www.oyez.org/justices

Supreme Court of the United States. "Harper v. Virginia Board of Elections. Oral Argument – January 25, 1966." Oyez.org. Web. 4 April 2017. https://apps.oyez.org/player/#/warren13/oral_argument_audio/15271

Supreme Court of the United States. "Harper v. Virginia Board of Elections. Oral Argument – January 26, 1966." Oyez.org. Web. 4 April 2017. https://apps.oyez.org/player/#/warren13/oral_argument_audio/15274

"Poll Tax." BallotPedia. Web. Accessed 4 April 2017. https://ballotpedia.org/Poll_tax

Chapter Nine

Jones, Michele Davis. "The Rules of the Game and Who Governs: Municipal Reform and Re-Reform in Norfolk, Virginia." University of Virginia. Department of Politics. May, 2006.

"Dr. Reid to be Installed." *Journal and Guide*, 29 Oct 1966, pg. 18.

"Red Carpet for 1,000 Visitors." *Journal and Guide*, 18 May 1968, pg. 2.

"Martin Luther King, Jr. and the Global Freedom Struggle: Poor People's Campaign." Stanford University, King Institute. Web. 21 Jul 2017. http://kingencyclopedia.stanford.edu/encyclopedia/encyclopedia/enc_poor_peoples_campaign/

"The American Presidency Project. Election of 1968." Gerhard Peters and John T. Woolley. 1999-2017. Web 21 Jul 2017. http://www.presidency.ucsb.edu/showelection.php?year=1968

"Wallace Finishes Poor 3rd." *The Virginian-Pilot*, 6 Nov 1968, pg. 21.

"Demo Election Headquarters Open." *Journal and Guide*, 2 Nov 1968, pg. B4.

"Campaign in Norfolk." *Journal and Guide*, 28 Sep 1968, pg. 1.

Jacox, Cal. "Aim: Build School on Present Site: Unity Campaign Seeks Over 10,000 Signatures." *Journal and Guide*, 13 Sep 1969, pg. A1.

"Negroes Aid in Primary Upsets: Byrd 'Machine' Kayoed As Voters Make History." *Journal and Guide*, 19 Jul 1969, pg. B23.

Spivack, Robert G. "Watch on the Potomac: New Politics in Va." *Journal and Guide*, 2 August 1969, pg. B10.

"Warning to Voters." *Journal and Guide* 30 Nov 1974, pg. 10.

Chapter Ten

Sweeney, James R. "Henry E. Howell (1920–1997)." Encyclopedia Virginia. Virginia Foundation for the Humanities, 8 Oct. 2015. Web. 21 Jul. 2017. https://www.encyclopediavirginia.org/Howell_ Henry_E_1920-1997

"Minister Elected to Head Norfolk's Urban Coalition." *Journal and Guide*, 9 Jan 1971, pg. 10.

Encyclopedia.chicagohistory.org (model cities program)

"Urges Public Prodding: Mrs. Green Calls CAC A "Do-Nothing" Group." *Journal and Guide*, 23 Jan 1965, pg. C1.

"Mrs. Butts Named to Uplift Unit." *The Virginian-Pilot*, 16 July 1975, pg. B8

Wood, William H. "New Member takes NHRA to task on Berkley housing." *The Virginian-Pilot*, 18 Nov 1975, pg. A1.

"Alfred and Evelyn show running again." *The Virginian-Pilot*. 9 Mar 1976, pg. B1.

Lake, Marvin Leon. "Butts reflects on her work with the NHRA." *The Virginian-Pilot*: Compass, 9 Aug 1987, pg. 4.

"New high-rise for elderly set." Ledger Star, 19 Dec 1977, pg. A4.

Miles, Winona S. "Norfolk Redevelopment and Housing Authority Activity Summary, 1974-1979." May, 1980.

"Staylor, Summers Rap King Memorial", *Journal and Guide*; Nov 1, 1975; pg. 1

Cox, Herman A., Jr. "Black Voice Ignored as NHRA Chooses New Head." *Journal and Guide*, 10 Dec 1977, pg. 1.

Stevens, Willie. "Looking on in Norfolk: Poor Folks Caught In Housing Mess." *Journal and Guide*, 3 January 1976, pg. 2.

Finney, Ava L. "Says Mrs. Carter: 'Jimmy Will Aid Minorities.'" *Journal and Guide*, 16 Oct 1976, pg. 2.

Goldberg, Steve. "Carter Wins in 3 Cities." *The Virginian-Pilot*, 3 Nov 1976, pg. A1

"270 to Win: 1976 Presidential Election." 270 to Win. 2004-2017. Web. 21 Jul 2017. http://www.270towin.com/1976_Election/

"Campaign for Reelection: Steering Committee For Del. Robinson Announced." *Journal and Guide*, 14 Aug 1971, pg. C1.

Coit, John. "She's on Party Line and Likes it Fine." *The Virginian-Pilot*, 7 Nov 1979, pg. A3.

Hunt, Don, Lake, Marvin Leon. "Black Vote Still Spells Defeat for Republicans." *The Virginian-Pilot*, 8 Nov 1979, pg. A1.

"Women of Virginia's 3rd Force to Honor Pres. Evelyn Butts." *Journal and Guide*, 30 November 1979, pg. 3.

Bernstein, Paul. "Mrs. Butts: Black Leader Eyes Council." *The Virginian-Pilot*, 19 Feb 1980, pg. C1.

Bernstein, Paul. "Goldenrod Lists Mrs. Butts, Mrs. Howell." *The Virginian-Pilot*, 4 May 1980, pg. B3.

Bernstein, Paul. "Mrs. Howell Top Winner in Norfolk." *The Virginian-Pilot*, 7 May 1980, pg. A1.

Bernstein, Paul. "Mr. Butts Attacks Howell Staff." *The Virginian-Pilot*, 8 May 1980, pg. A1.

"Norfolk delegate hospitalized." Ledger Star, 14 Aug 1980, pg. A2

Dingle, Derek T. "Roslyn Carter in Huntersville." *Journal and Guide*, 1 Oct 1980, pg. 1.

Dingle, Derek T. "Virginians Mourn Loss of Powerful Politician." *Journal and Guide*, 21 January 1981, pg. 1.

"Robinson is Newest Delegate." *Journal and Guide*, 11 Feb 1981, pg. 1.

"A Saturday Morning Campaign." *Journal and Guide*, 21 October 1981, pg. 1.

Chapter Eleven

Yancey, D. "Charles S. "Chuck" Robb." Encyclopedia Virginia. Virginia Foundation for the Humanities, 5 Jan. 2014. Web. 21 Jul. 2017. https://www.encyclopediavirginia.org/Robb_Charles_S_1939-

Veth, Steven G. "Minister with vision sought 'seat at the table.'" *The Virginian-Pilot*, 21 Feb 2009, pg. A1

Parramore, Thomas C., Stewart, Peter C., Bogger, Tommy L. Norfolk: The First Four Centuries. Charlottesville: University Press of Virginia, 1994.

Littlejohn, Jeffrey L., Ford, Charles H. Elusive Equality: Desegregation and Resegregation in Norfolk. Charlottesville: University Press of Virginia, 2010.

"Mrs. Butts appointed to board." *The Virginian-Pilot*, 3 Jul 1982, pg. B2.

James, Alfreda. "Dr. Miller Files With 500 Names." *Journal and Guide*, 6 Apr 1983, pg. 1.

Fiske, Warren. "Lacking blacks, agency is turned down." *The Virginian-Pilot*, 8 Mar 1983, pg. C3.

Fiske, Warren. "Leaders celebrate Waterside opening." *The Virginian-Pilot*, 1 Jun 1981, pg. A1.

Interview with Yvonne Miller by Charlene Ligon. October 2007.

Fiske, Warren. "Mrs. Butts is in race to stay." *The Virginian-Pilot*, 19 Feb 1984, pg. B1.

Fiske, Warren. "Willis, Butts exchange angry words." *The Virginian-Pilot*, 27 Apr 1984, pg. B2.

Fiske, Warren. "Butts receives letter from Robb, biracial support." *The Virginian-Pilot*, 25 Apr 1984, pg. C1.

Fiske, Warren. "White group gives support to Evelyn Butts." *The Virginian-Pilot*, 24 Apr 1984, pg. C1

Fiske, Warren. "Irony, complexity mark council race." *The Virginian-Pilot*, 22 Apr 1984, pg. B1.

Fiske, Warren. "Foster is second black on council." *The Virginian-Pilot*, 2 May 1984, pg. A1.

Wilder, L. Douglas. Son of Virginia: A Life in America's Political Arena. Guilford, Connecticut: Lyone Press, 2015.

Schreuder, Cindy. "Forces of Butts, Willis clash again." *The Virginian-Pilot*, 4 Dec 1985, pg. D1

Jones, Michele Davis. "The Rules of the Game and Who Governs: Municipal Reform and Re-Reform in Norfolk, Virginia." University of Virginia. Department of Politics. May, 2006.

Jenkins, Kent, Jr. "Canada aided by forces tied to Democrat Butts." *The Virginian-Pilot*, 5 Nov 1986, pg. 1.

Novek, Ellie. "Butts, Willis in forefront as races shape up: 2 leaders of blacks may compete for turf." *The Virginian-Pilot*, 5 Apr 1987, pg. B1.

Chapter Twelve

Swift, Earl. "Democrats reject longtime activist Butts." *Virginian-Pilot*, 6 Dec 1987, pg. B1.

Swift, Earl. "Lonely: Burned bridges backfire for Butts." *The Virginian-Pilot*: Compass, 17 Apr 1988, pg. 6.

"Who is Lyndon LaRouche?" Executive Intelligence Review. Web 21 Jul 2017. http://www.larouchepub.com/larouche_biography.html

"Atlantic National Bank faces uphill battle: Heavy financial loss during 3-month period." *Journal and Guide*, 28 Sep 1988, pg. 1.

Colvin, Leonard. "Confederate flag: what does it mean?" *Journal and Guide*, 9 Mar 1988, pg. 1.

Lyles, Charlise. "Lawyers are urged to serve the poor." *The Virginian-Pilot*, 2 May 1989, pg. D4.

"A Broadcast Empire in Decline: L.E. Willis Sr. has had legal and other woes in recent years." *The Virginian-Pilot*, 24 Nov 1993, pg. A2.

Colvin, Leonard. "Joe Jordan Foundation will head efforts to build M.L.K. memorial." *Journal and Guide*, 2 Aug 1989, pg. 1.

Colvin, Leonard. "Martin Luther King memorial in Norfolk still only a dream." *New Journal and Guide*, 29 Jul 1992, pg. 1.

Golden, Ron. "Black Media Professionals honor own with awards." *Journal and Guide*, 31 Jan 1990, pg. 1.

Swift, Earl. "Era Ends: Black coalition ousts longtime leader." *The Virginian-Pilot*, 10 Jun 1990, pg. B1.

Colvin, Leonard Essau. "Concerned Citizens seek revitalization." *Journal and Guide*, 13 Jun 1990, pg. 1.

"73 Years later, it's wards?" *The Virginian-Pilot*, Compass, 4 Nov 1990, pg. 12.

Knepler, Mike, and Suo, Steve. "How will Black voter greet ward system? Leaders debate alignments." *The Virginian-Pilot*, Compass, 4 Nov 1990, pg. 10.

Swift, Earl. "James Gay awaits kidney transplant, chance at new life." *The Virginian-Pilot*, 7 Jan 2007.

Bogger, Tommy. "History of Norfolk Project Transcript: Oral Interview of Judge Joseph Jordan." 31 May 1989

Germanotta, Tony. "Civil Rights leader Jordan dies at 67. Was pioneer on Norfolk City Council." *The Virginian-Pilot*, 15 Jun 1991, pg. A1.

Colvin, Leonard. "Remembering the legendary Jordan." *Journal and Guide*, 19 Jun 1991, pg. 1.

Huang, Thomas. "Hundreds pay tribute to Evelyn Butts." *The Virginian-Pilot*, 20 March 1993, pg. D1.

Colvin, Leonard. "Area mourns for Evelyn Butts: She fought for, won case to end poll tax." *New Journal and Guide*, 17 Mar 1993, pg. 1.

Epilogue

Marshall, Alex. "Black officials split from coalition. Willis' leadership style is blamed for the group's division." *The Virginian-Pilot*, 2 May 1995, pg. B4.

Colvin, Leonard. "Political wind blows in Norfolk. Rainbow Coalition defectors return to coalition founded by Evelyn Butts." *New Journal and Guide* (1916-2003), 3 May 1995, pg. 1.

Colvin, Leonard. "Collins gets Council to re-name Elm St. for Mrs. Evelyn Butts." *New Journal and Guide* , 9 Aug 1995, pg. 1.

Knepler, Mike. "Reforming democracy. nti-poll ta legacy lives on today. Butts' fight part of campaign-finance reform." *Virginian Pilot*, 26 Feb 2001, pg. A1

Swift, Earl. "20 Tidewater Titans." *The Virginian-Pilot*, 31 Dec 1999, pg. A2.

"Too poor to vote: how Alabama's 'new poll tax' bars thousands of people from voting" theguardian.com web. 2017 October 2004 https://amp.theguardian.com/us-news/2017/oct/04/alabama-voting-poll-tax.

INDEX

INDEX

INDEX

INDEX

INDEX

INDEX

INDEX

INDEX

INDEX

INDEX

INDEX

INDEX